Surviving the Line of Duty

SURVIVING THE LINE OF DUTY

DANIEL BARBA

XULON PRESS

Xulon Press
2301 Lucien Way #415
Maitland, FL 32751
407.339.4217
www.xulonpress.com

© 2021 by Dan Barba

All rights reserved solely by the author. The author guarantees all contents are original and do not infringe upon the legal rights of any other person or work. No part of this book may be reproduced in any form without the permission of the author.

Due to the changing nature of the Internet, if there are any web addresses, links, or URLs included in this manuscript, these may have been altered and may no longer be accessible. The views and opinions shared in this book belong solely to the author and do not necessarily reflect those of the publisher. The publisher therefore disclaims responsibility for the views or opinions expressed within the work.

Unless otherwise indicated, Scripture quotations taken from the Holy Bible, New International Version (NIV). Copyright © 1973, 1978, 1984, 2011 by Biblica, Inc.™. Used by permission. All rights reserved.

Scripture quotations taken from the King James Version (KJV)–*public domain*.

Paperback ISBN-13: 978-1-66282-976-5
Ebook ISBN-13: 978-1-66282-977-2

TABLE OF CONTENTS

Introduction: *First Responders* vii

Chapter 1: This Can't Be Real 1

Chapter 2: End of Watch: A Sacrifice 23

Chapter 3: Life on the Rubber Gun Squad and Wandering in the Wilderness 45

Chapter 4: Reinstatement, Eye of the Tiger 65

Chapter 5: Change of Scenery and Promotion . . . 91

Chapter 6: Transfer Back to Santa Maria and Looking Evil in the Eye 111

Chapter 7: Back to the Rubber Gun Squad 127

Chapter 8: Retirement 143

Chapter 9: The Situation at Home 153

Conclusion: *The Age of Defund* 157

I was that which others did not want to be.
I went where others feared to go,
and did what others failed to do.
I asked nothing from those who gave nothing,
and reluctantly accepted the thought of eternal loneliness...
should I fail.
I have seen the face of terror, felt the stinging cold of fear;
and enjoyed the sweet taste of a moment's love...
I have cried, pained, and hoped...but most of all,
I have lived times others would say were best forgotten.
At least someday I will be able to say that I was proud of what I was
...a soldier...of the law. - Author Unknown

This book takes the reader into the patrol car and out onto the streets to experience some of the most horrifying events imaginable. Instead of a single event, this is a series of events that span four different decades. It is a real view into why so many first responders end up suiciding. There is no study, no survey, just the reality of life for first responders and the magnitude of the forgiveness and miracles of the Lord Jesus Christ and how He can turn misery into joy.

Introduction

First Responders

Today, we see so much attention focused on "first responders." It's a broad term, but who are first responders? This list is by no means exhaustive, but it sheds a light on just how many people are involved: Law enforcement, fire, ambulance personnel, dispatchers, tow truck drivers, doctors, nurses, ER technicians, therapists (who help pick up the pieces, as we shall see), and any support personnel. Even if you are involved on the periphery, you are a first responder.

Many first responders not only risk their lives daily, but their mental wellbeing as well. For many of us, the damage, the fallout, and the price our families pay only begin when the event is over.

The following are events as I experienced them. I believe they are proof of God's existence and the fact that He loves us and sent His Son to die for us. I believe it is also proof that God has sent not only medical doctors, but licensed mental health professionals who are instrumental in helping us through the dark times.

I asked coworkers and others who were at many of the scenes and events I will be talking about, what they saw, and if the way I am portraying them is accurate. We all see and experience things differently. I have done my due diligence to ensure I am portraying my experiences as accurately as possible, but again, these are my experiences. This is what happened to me. This is my descent into a living hell and how the Lord Jesus Christ reached down and not only saved me, but gave me purpose and enabled me to use my experiences to help others who were or are heading into the place I was.

My purpose? My purpose is simple: get the attention of any first responders or anybody who honors me by taking the time to read this and is at or near the end of the road and lead them to salvation through Christ.

> **I do not want to pull anyone into a denominational box or bore them with dogma, but a new life better than you could imagine through salvation and inspiring them to use your experiences to help those you serve with**

Chapter 1

THIS CAN'T BE REAL

MYSELF

I WAS BORN AND RAISED (7TH GENERATION) in San Luis Obispo, California, in 1965. My parents raised my sister and me in a very strict evangelical household. My father was a police officer on SLOPD and my mother was a regional deli-bakery supervisor for a large grocery chain.

I accepted Christ as my savior as a very young kid. I cannot stress it enough that God is not only a God of deliverance (He can save you no matter what age or what horrible circumstances you are in), but He is also a God of protection. As His child, He can protect you (see Psalm 91:7) no matter where He sends you.

I always felt He was taking care of me, especially as I entered the California Highway Patrol Academy in 1989, against my father's wishes. I saw God move in many ways as a child and an adult, through miracles and answered prayers. My parents definitely showed me the way to go and the Lord did the rest. I had a wonderful, carefree childhood and felt very blessed. I didn't want it to end and fought growing up, but became very naive and sheltered.

> **Consequently, I was not nearly prepared for the streets and freeways of Los Angeles when I was sent there straight out of the academy in the Fall of 1989.**

This Can't Be Real

Upon arriving at my first station with seven fellow cadets, I could tell my backward, innocent (whatever you want to call it) ways were of big entertainment to the officers and sergeants who were there. The jokes and cartoons were actually funny and well deserved. I felt it was their form of acceptance and amusement.

All my field training officers were motorcycle officers. Sort of an elite group and I was to go through the same initiation that everyone else did, to see if I could take a career of more than just chasing taillights.

Other than the many aspects of break-in training on the CHP, the one I dreaded most was going through the Los Angeles County Medical Examiner's Office. It's a place where bodies of young and old go who have not had a cause of death established, or who die outside the hospital and have not yet been claimed by family or loved ones.

I was the first of my seven fellow rookies to go on my "Tour." My FTO and I were planning on eating at the McDonalds across the street when we were done.

As we walked up to the big steel door, I heard a heavy "CLUNK" as the door rolled back and opened. I was immediately hit with a wretched, horrible stench with a sort of sweet twist to it. I knew what it was but was too scared to stand still or walked in. On the floor in front of me was a black body bag that had a multicolored slime draining out into the floor drain. My FTO and I walked past it and another door opened and an even stronger odor hit me. Down the hallway in front of me were dead people, some on gurneys some on the floor, and some even stacked on top of each other. I could not believe what I was seeing. It was at that moment that I just kept telling myself, "this is not real," over and over; anything to make it out of there without losing it and running out the door.

Off to my right was a worker at a desk eating a sandwich. Another person came out from another door gowned up with heavy gloves on. Upon seeing me standing there she said, "Oh good. Someone to help me pull some of them down." She took us into a massive cooler that had a bit more pleasant, but acrid smell. I could see large bunks/racks that lined the walls, full of bodies in clear bags, stacked on top of each other. The floor was full of gurneys, some with multiple bodies. The tops of the racks had large semi see-through jars that contained aborted and miscarried babies.

My tour guide then took me to the homicide room. It also stunk to high heaven. It was filled almost beyond capacity. Most were young, juvenile gangsters and still had some or all of their "colors." Some had their shirts cut or torn open revealing multiple gunshots or stab wounds. I was looking into the faces of junior high and high school kids. Their eyes were half open and looking up as if they had been looking for a way out but couldn't find one out of a life trapped on the streets and the dead-end of gang life. I happened to look at several of their toe tags and I noticed that instead of names, most had "John Doe or Jane Doe" written on them. The families couldn't or wouldn't claim them. I was overwhelmed by sadness and wondered if anyone cared for these kids.

The worst thing of all was I felt something evil in the room and it was laughing. It had won. It had claimed these little ones and was rejoicing.

I have never thought of myself as a spiritual powerhouse, but I could actually feel an evil presence that seemed to be gloating over its trophies. That feeling went away as soon as we walked into and quickly out of the decomp room. I can't describe that place.

I soon found myself standing in a room, watching an autopsy on a small child. I was told to get closer and walked within 3 feet of the table. I watched the medical examiner remove its organs and brain. By then, I was on overload and thankfully at the end of my one-hour tour.

Needless to say, we were not hungry for McDonald's or anything else for that fact. My uniform stunk so bad, I had to take it off. I couldn't get the smell of rotting human flesh off it or out of my nose. I did not sleep for three days and two nights. I had no place to put all that I had seen. I could not go back to work and show any kind of negative impact or distress from the experience because I knew it would be viewed as a weakness by my new peers. So, I stuffed it down. I had plenty of room, after all.

Nice Guys Are Convenient Targets

The station I transferred to was very small. There were twelve to fifteen officers, two sergeants, and a lieutenant commander. The officers were all first-rate guys and very senior with a few exceptions. You never had to ask for backup or help because it was already there.

Out of these, there were only four of us who were churchgoers: me, two Mormons, and a Baptist.

There could have been more, but they never came forward. The four of us were very kind-hearted and non-confrontational.

Our lieutenant commander was, many people felt, an evil person who delighted in human mental suffering and anguish. He always needed someone to literally persecute, and he took his time doing it.

> **One of the old, grizzled veterans told him, "Our lives are in more danger in the station than out in the streets because we come in here and our blood pressure goes up, we are on edge and afraid, and we never know who you are going to victimize next."**

I recall shortly after transferring into this particular station, I was told that it was open warfare with the commander and one of his sergeants. On my first day, the commander told me he kept a notebook on everyone, and I would be no exception. Every time he heard or saw something, he would write it down. What he didn't know was that the squad did the same to him.

My third day was a training day, and the fur flew. The commander let them all know he returned several hundred hours of grant overtime to HQ. He seemed to enjoy the yelling and instigating all the anger that he triggered. I got a real evil vibe from him. Never before and never since have I ever gotten such a heavy seething, evil feeling from a coworker or from someone else who wore a badge.

I was told by officers from bordering stations that because I had a Hispanic surname, I would soon become a target. I noticed that the persecution really was aimed at those who were kind-hearted and had some kind of church affiliation. I did hear and see things pointed at Hispanics as well (our station was in a major agricultural area of Santa Barbara County).

The commander and his sergeant would make comments when hit and run accidents would come out on the radio like, "Must be some dumb beaner that did it" or "You could be out in the field picking strawberries" if anybody objected or voiced the most minor complaints.

When the seatbelt law came into effect, the commander would have his sergeant literally follow us out of the office to the agricultural fields and parts of town where the Mexican field laborers worked and lived. They would oversee and force those of us on dayshift to cite the field workers. This was not done to any other part of the valley. One month, I was a bit low on my seatbelt citation quota. I told the sergeant that I was looking very hard, but I felt the buckle-up campaign was working. He told me, "go cite the Mexicans they never wear their seatbelts." Apparently, he did not see the Mexican last name on my nameplate. More info on this later.

The focused persecution took other forms. On a particular afternoon shift, one of our very senior officers, who the sergeant absolutely despised, received a phone call. His adult son had been involved in some sort of industrial accident and the prognosis was not good. He told the sergeant what had happened and he needed to leave immediately. The sergeant said no and told him to stay and finish his shift. This officer had well over twenty years in the department, but would be routinely brought into the sergeant's office. It happened nearly every day and forced him to go over the previous day's dispatch tapes because his tone of voice was not right or something in his radio broadcasts were "very bad." No other guy on the beat could think of a single thing the guy had done wrong.

When nothing could be found on us, things were fabricated. I stopped and ticketed a guy twice for speeding within one hour. He filed a citizen's complaint on me alleging he told me he was having a heart attack. It never happened. I told the sergeant the truth that it never happened. When the sergeant printed his findings, he said that I had confessed to him that indeed the man was having a heart attack and I felt it was a ploy to get out of the citation. I adamantly denied this in front of him and the lieutenant (who put him up to it). I even offered to take a polygraph. The lieutenant hated the sergeant's guts and even though he had told him to do what he did, he decided to have some fun and asked the sergeant in front of me and my union representative if I really did make those stunning admissions. The sergeant actually said no that I did not make those admissions.

Wow! I thought I was home free. The truth had come out and would be exonerated. Not so fast. My union rep told me the lieutenant was going to sustain it against me anyway and not change any of the findings because he felt like it. It was not until a lengthy appeal process that the lieutenant and the sergeant were forced by their superiors to reverse the findings. Nothing punitive was done to the lieutenant or sergeant. It was at that point I knew all their actions were actually condoned.

Can you imagine literally scrapping bodies of adults and children off the pavement and taking abuse from the public only to be persecuted and witch-hunted by our commanders? It would get worse. Much worse. I had never had an enemy in my life until this point in my career.

On top of dealing with the nonstop bloodshed and mayhem, I was experiencing a new emotion. The simple sight of the commander and his sergeant elicited a visceral, seething, unbridled, hatred within me. I would actually have dreams at night of physical harm befalling the both of them. I couldn't help my dreams, but I could help the hatred I felt for both of them.

> ***Can someone who claims Christ as savior really hate another person?***

You bet! I loved feeding on it. I loved chiming in with the old veterans, other officers, and officers from other stations at coffee how much we hated the lieutenant and sergeant. The two of them were very well known and almost legendary far and wide for their prosecutorial methods and gross incompetence.

One hot day, a guy I worked with found a very needy family whose car had broken down on a remote road about 10 miles out of town. He was on duty and saw they could not afford any repairs to their car. He drove into town, got the right part, ran home, and got some tools. Though he will not admit it, he bought them some food, too. He went back and fixed their car without neglecting his duties and got them on their way.

The same commander found out what he had done and became very angry. He felt it was far too much, but moreover, he detested the act of kindness. He began to persecute the officer relentlessly for years until the officer finally retired because of the stress.

The commander would see some of us struggle with the traumatic events on the streets and would go out of his way to make sure he and his sergeant piled on more and more. For example, they would make sure I was assigned to the highest traffic collision beat when beats were always alternated daily. I ended up working this beat a solid month taking thirty-one traffic collision reports when the normal picture was three to five for the month.

An officer who worked a desk job told me the commander and his sergeant were out to get me and the other meeker officers. The sergeant had actually told him so and he had also overheard them talking and plotting.

The Ripple Effect

Near Thanksgiving of 1991, I was working in an unincorporated area of northern Santa Barbara County. My dispatcher was a veteran dispatcher of twenty-plus years. She dispatched me to an injury accident using the usual "10" code with my unit designator 14-11, never using names.

This time, her voice cracked as she said, "Dan….this is a bad one."

It felt like my heart stopped and I felt nauseous, but I flipped on my lights and siren and went as fast as I could, being the first on the scene. I saw what seemed like endless lines of skid marks that terminated at a sedan that was incredibly wrapped around a pole. I ran up to the car and put my head through the spot where the right window used to be. I first looked to my right and saw a young seventeen-year-old girl that looked like she had been thrown up under the dash. Physics and high-speed accidents do not mix.

As I turned my head to my left to look in the back seat where the car had impacted the pole, I came nearly face to face with a fourteen-month-old-child, still in her chair with brain matter hanging out of her nose. I was trying to cope with what I was looking at and I do not remember the fire department or the ambulance arriving. I just remember a paramedic looking in the car and yelling, "I can't do anything about that! I can't do anything about that!"

The fire department had most of the car's roof peeled off and the teen driver pulled out from under the dash and onto the front seat, beginning CPR. She had the thousand-yard stare and I tried to get away by moving slightly, but it seemed that wherever I went, she was staring right through me. I watched as her life ebbed away, as the medics and firemen fought as hard as they could to save her. Her injuries were too severe and she was declared dead at the scene.

I have tried to forget what I saw, but it is with me to this day. The driver turned out to be the child's aunt.

Fast forward seven years. I was working in a very remote area of northeastern Santa Barbara County. It was so remote we had to refuel our Mustang patrol cars at the local Cal-Trans yard. The state Cal-Trans workers actually lived out at the yard in trailers.

I was gassing up my Mustang at the pumps when this CalTrans worker came out of his trailer and we started talking. I could tell he had a rough life and his face looked like he had been a heavy drinker. He asked me what my worst experience had been and I began to tell him about this incident. I noticed his eyes began to tear up. He stopped me and said that the driver was his daughter and I assumed the child was his granddaughter.

This man was an acquaintance of mine for several years. I wondered many times why his physical appearance looked like he was a heavy drinker. We have no idea what each person is carrying and many people, particularly our youth, do not think about the long-reaching effects of our decisions, like that young girl going so very fast. Our present generation of young people live in a "do-over" mentality. When they die in one of their video games, they just push "do-over", or they have nine lives left and that mentality can carry over into their everyday lives and consequences last forever sometimes.

Like all my traumatic incidents, the sights and sounds of this particular tragedy are burned into my mind.

> **Though I was stuffing it down, I had the Lord next to me as I walked this journey. The father/grandfather of these girls did not. I do not ever remember seeing him again. Who was there helping him carry his burdens?**

Playing God

Approximately one month after that double tragedy, I found myself on Christmas Day 1991 working a fairly remote part of the 101 freeway. There were only two of us for the entire shift. About a quarter of a mile south of me I saw a large pillar of dust go up in the air. I rushed over to the scene and my eyes met a horrible sight. I saw a Dodge Colt approximately 4 feet in the air wrapped around a very large oak tree. The entire front of the car from the dashboard forward was missing. It had been torn off with the engine and flew 250 feet north of the rest of the car with its headlights still on.

I grabbed my large EMT bag and ran up. Again, I was the only person there. (not many people on the road on Christmas back then). I saw a twenty-something-year-old woman at the wheel, obviously dead. I will spare my reader the details, but it was awful. I saw two boys ages four and five years of age. One had been ejected and was not breathing. He had a strong heartbeat but gruesome signs of a massive head injury. The boy still inside the car was trapped in a pocket behind his dead mother, with his head impaled with a piece of trim from the vehicle. He was fully conscious, screaming, and thrashing around. I could barely reach him and could not hold him still.

In the academy, we can train you for a lot, but we cannot train you or prepare you to be God! I was an EMT and an officer. I had people counting on me to make the right call. I was trained in triage and even surprised myself at how fast I made my decision. The child who was not breathing needed me the most. I could not fully reach the one in the car. From his horrible screams, I could tell he could breathe. I hooked his brother up to oxygen and began breathing for him. Meanwhile, the screams from the car lessened and stopped.

In those days, we did not have paramedics with our county fire department. I was on my own for about 15-20 very long minutes. I recall the county fire's arrival. It was a very long extrication. The scene was too much for one of the firemen and he went on stress leave and retired within a day or two. I felt so bad for him, but I was really struggling, too. Did it all just build up and was this the final incident that did it?

I tried so very hard to save the one child that I did not notice a large amount of his blood all over my uniform, my arms, and my radio. I was told the child in the car did make it, then did not. I still do not know to this day.

By this time, the other officer had arrived along with the on-call sergeant, who I will talk about later. He called both of us together and began to chew us out for, in his opinion, improper traffic control. He had to have seen the blood all over me, the dead bodies at the scene, and the bewildered looks on our faces, but chose to ignore it. Treatment like this was commonplace in that station, especially to kind-hearted officers and those who were known to be churchgoers.

I could not hold still for hours after the incident. I had to just move. Move until the scenes of the day began to subside. I would not, could not go to the elephant in the room.

> **I had to play God and choose between two kids. As the thought began to creep in, I felt something that I could not control, block it and wipe it out of my mind.**

It was not until Christmas day three or four years later when I found myself on the floor of my shower curled up in a ball with the warm water hitting me, crying uncontrollably, that the fact hit me. I **had to choose**, and what made it worse was that it was two children.

Helpless

Not long after, I was working the swing shift on the 101 freeway. It was around 8:30 at night and I saw a large glow a few miles away, east of the freeway. I knew it was a fire and I knew it had to be a structure because there was nothing around to burn that bad.

Within 1 minute, I rolled up to a gate and saw a large farmhouse nearly fully engulfed. I put it out on the radio and, as usual, I was the first on the scene. A lady came running out from nowhere and yelled that there were two small boys trapped in the house. The house was about a quarter of a mile from the road. I came rolling up to the house and could feel the intense heat and had to back the patrol car up. My plan was to throw my large CHP coat over me and run up and into the front door because I could still see it and maybe the kids were near the door. I got out and the heat was so intense, I knew I could not get within 100 feet of it.

At that moment, the first fire engine pulled right up to me. I looked up and yelled at the fire captain that there were two small boys still in the house. From the glow on the front of the fire engine cab, I could see him and the engineer, who was also looking at me, suddenly and simultaneously look up at the house and just stared. The stare seemed like a long time, but I could read the looks on their faces. I already knew it anyway. There was absolutely no way anything could survive in that inferno. I just hoped they died of smoke inhalation and not the horrible flames.

> **I knew there was nothing anybody could do, but I still felt helpless. I was a first responder. I was supposed to be able to dash in and save them. The firemen were supposed to dash in and save them.**

Hardly any words were spoken the entire time we were out on the scene. I could tell those the firemen felt the same. The next day, they did find the boys' bodies up near the front door.

Holiday Assignments

Because of my low seniority, I worked many holidays. I totally understood that. When Thanksgiving and Christmas would roll around and you would normally be stationed on a beat that was close to or in the area you lived, you were allowed to keep sweeping your beat every hour or so and then go to your house but keep your radio on you. If you lived outside the area, it did not matter where you worked. On most of those holidays, I would be assigned to the only beat that we did not always staff seventy-five or eighty miles from my house and forty-five to fifty miles out of town.

On one occasion, with the help of a federal park employee and two other friends, I rescued twenty-two high school students in the snowy hills of Santa Barbara County. I was two hours late getting back to the station, racking up some overtime. I would end up getting a letter of commendation from the principal of that school, but all I got from my sergeant (the same one who chewed me out in that Christmas day 1991 fatality accident) was getting yelled at, "You're late!"

Brave Little Girl

Some of the biggest lessons we learn are from kids.

One particular dayshift, I was working the 101 freeway again in northern Santa Barbara County when a call went out over the air that a group of off duty sheriff deputies carpooling on their way home, came upon a vehicle that went off the roadway, off the edge, and into some large oak trees 50 feet below.

As I pulled up, the deputies came up the hill and advised me that there were three dead: an adult male, an adult female, and a twelve-year-old girl. The ambulance was loading up a four-year-old girl with a major head injury. One whole side of her face was crushed, but she was fully conscious. I performed my duties at the scene, but I wanted to vomit looking at the victims and dreaded going to the hospital to check on the little girl.

I arrived at the hospital and went into the emergency room where this little girl was being treated. The doctor warned me she looked bad with one whole side of her face crushed. However, what he could not believe was that she was so calm and talking, asking about her daddy.

There were no witnesses to this crash and this little girl was the only one who could tell me anything about it. I quickly learned she was asleep when it happened, but more so, the man driving was not her father. All she could tell me was that her daddy drove trains. Unknowingly, she described listening to her twelve-year-old sister die in the car. It took about a half-hour, but I located her father about 50 miles away at work as a railroad engineer.

I know it was the Lord who kept me calm, but I told him there had been an accident and he needed to get to the hospital ASAP. He kept asking about his family. I felt bad but told him they were still being worked on (which they actually were) and to just get here.

During this time, the previously mentioned sergeant had been called in due to the magnitude of the incident. The father arrived and began to fill in the blanks. During this time, the doctors and nursing staff had learned what had happened and were very emotional. The sergeant told me he was unable to tell the man that his wife and twelve-year-old daughter had been killed in an accident by another man. He followed me into the room where the father was seated. I used a very low tone as he leaned forward. I put my hand on his left shoulder and told him what had happened. He sunk to the floor and began to wail. I cannot convey to you how awful it is to witness such human suffering and distress. I looked back and my sergeant was crying heavily. It turns out that he and his wife were estranged, and the driver was her boyfriend. He was on probation and not supposed to travel outside San Bernardino County.

Once the father could partway recover enough to see his little girl, I told him how she would look. We went in and there were a lot of nursing staff and doctors. My sergeant was right behind me, still crying along with everyone else. I knew I had to hold it together and again, it was only the Lord who helped me.

The little girl had just been told her mother and sister had died and she calmly said she was glad that she lived so, "Now I can take care of my daddy." Everyone in the room really lost it then! I barely kept it together. I could feel a single tear flow down my right cheek.

It was at this time, I saw a rare gesture from my sergeant who I thought was mean, cold, and unfeeling. He came up and actually put his arm around me and said how proud he was of me and for me to go back to the station and take the rest of the day off. Of course, none of my behavior he was proud of ever made my monthly evaluation, but my opinion of him changed that day a bit for the better. It meant a lot to me. Even though he would later still try to pile things on me, I actually felt my hatred of him lift.

Guide to Surviving in the Line of Duty

At the end of each chapter, I will share suggestions to help you deal with the emotional roller coaster after experiencing trauma or tragedy in your own personal line of duty.

I had no place to put all that I had seen. I tried to forget it all by stuffing it down.

Does this describe how you are handling your own emotional trauma?

Though I was stuffing it down, I had the Lord next to me as I walked this journey.

Who is helping you carry your emotional burdens?

Read John 3:16-17 and Psalm 23:4.

I believe God loves us and sent His Son to die for us.

Will you accept His gift of love and salvation?

I also believe God has sent medical doctors and licensed mental health professionals who are instrumental in helping us through the dark times.

Chapter 2

END OF WATCH: A SACRIFICE

"Greater love hath no man than this: that a man lay down his life for his friends."
(John 15:13)

YOU CAN TELL BY THIS TITLE THAT THIS DOES not end well.

All of you first responders know what shift work is like and how, especially in your early years, you are constantly trading shifts swapping this day for that day. We have busy lives. How quickly we forget that none of us are 100 percent sure we are going to live to go home to our families at the end of a shift. We forget or do not think about the fire we are playing with and what could happen.

I recall a time when I first transferred into Santa Maria where I asked one of the veteran guys to trade a shift. I was shocked when he said no. I asked why and he said that nobody knows what's going to happen on a shift and he would only work the days he was scheduled for because if something did happen, it was meant to be. He knew. I was not upset in the least, but shocked because I realized what he said was a huge truth.

Before I go any further, I would like to introduce you to two of the best who ever pinned on the badge: Ricky Stovall and Britt Irvine. Both, senior to me, Ricky was a huge outdoorsman who was a top-level freediver, one heck of a fisherman with an awesome boat, and the best hunting partner you could ask for, ready at a moment's notice for whatever was in season. I think all tolled, he took most of our station out fishing at one time or another. But the biggest thing of all, Ricky was the best family man. I spent many graveyard shifts with him. He always told me how proud he was of his kids, how much he loved them, and how he absolutely adored his wife. I loved watching them interact. I have a memory of most nights I worked with him, he would tuck a small Gideons Bible in the visor of our patrol car.

Britt Irvine was an absolute man's man. Hands down, the most athletic guy in the station. He was a competitive swimmer the entire time I knew him in a very large city club as well as a member of a soccer club team. An avid water skier, he was once ranked in the top 7 in the world in the class he competed. Britt had a charisma about him that everybody loved and he didn't know a stranger. The biggest thing about him was he cared very deeply for his beat partners. One day, about a week before my wedding, I was a nervous wreck and it really showed. As soon as the briefing was over he told me to meet him at one of our coffee hangouts. We sat and he listened to how nervous I was. He gave me awesome advice and wrote his phone number on a scrap of paper and handed it to me and said if I needed anything, to call him at any hour. I also recall a time he was having a very hard time with a fatality crash he took that involved the death of a small child. In the station parking lot, I read him Matthew 19:14 where Christ showed how much he loved and cared for children and that how much his kingdom is based on the faith of a child. I told him the child may not be in the arms of the parents anymore, but he was now in the arms of our heavenly father. I could see this touched him deeply. He said, "words can't describe how much I believe in that book and everything in it". I passed many a graveyard shift with him. It never seemed like work. The shift always seemed to fly by.

February 1998 found me working the graveyard shift. The CHP doubles up two officers per car on the graveyard shift. Our area only had two graveyard units. Our station was so small, we only had 15-20 officers for all shifts. Typically, the officers would do the schedule. The two graveyard units would coordinate what days off each wanted, but it had to meet the approval of the sergeant who was in charge of scheduling.

I recall it was a very big El Nino year and California was getting hammered with rain and snow. My wife and I had planned a four-day snow trip, but I could only get three days off. I would have to engineer a swap with the other two guys in the other car. It was an indirect swap with some horse-trading. My partner and I would pay the other guys back later in the month.

I recall that it was raining and snowing so hard that we could not leave on the day we wanted. The last possible day came for us to be able to leave and it was still too messy outside and up on the slopes. I decided to call dispatch and tell them to let the other car know that I would be coming in. It then occurred to me that my partner had probably already made plans. I had picked up the phone and got the dial tone, but then hung up. I went to bed and didn't wake up until the next morning when my wife came running in crying.

She said that the guys who were working for me were missing. They had been dispatched out Highway 166 where the Cuyama River had washed the road out and several vehicles including a big rig had been washed into the river.

I remember trying to wake up and sort it out all at once. I sat on the edge of the bed. I knew it was not going to end well and I knew it was my fault. I saw my duty weapon on the dresser and the thought occurred to me, "Do it now and you won't have to go through what's coming." Had I not been raised in a good devout

Christian home and taught how suicide was not God's will, I would have done it.

I managed to get out to the living room and spent the next several hours watching the non-stop coverage on the local station. Pretty soon the call came in to respond to the station and wait for news there.

Two counties of search and rescue were out looking. Our dayshift guys were out there, too, with the shift sergeant. Two of the guys were combat veterans from Vietnam. It was getting dark and the order had come down for them to come back to the station. Both of them refused. They both said they never left anyone behind in the jungles of Vietnam and they weren't leaving until the guys were found. They would stay true to their word and bring their brothers back.

Those of us at the station were all saying how if anyone could survive a rushing river, it was these two. One was a world-class water skier (7th in the world at one time) and the other was a very accomplished spearfisherman. We were all sure they would be found clinging to a rock or log, but we all knew the truth. Hope was in short supply.

I was in the special duty office with another officer when the official word came down. The other officer had been reading and had his glasses on. They said our helicopter had spotted a tire sticking out of the mud. They found the guys' patrol car upside down in the river mud. The valiant search and rescue guys were working in the dark, digging to see if the guys were still in the car. Our worst fears came true. They were still on duty, seat-belted in their seats, so sadly, they were dead. The other officer looked at me, silently as tears just began streaming down his face.

By now, all the big shots and their minions started arriving, along with others who the guys had worked with over the years. The public began arriving, too. There was an absolute sea of flowers, cards, stuffed animals, you name it.

> **Lots and lots of folks from the entire area came. I would say to the public, this means more than words can express.**

Many times, we are not allowed to express anything publicly, but this showed that our community had our backs. Thank you all once again. I don't think any of us will forget it.

Our peer support unit showed up. It was the first I had ever heard of this group. It was a group of uniformed and non-uniformed people from the department who had been involved in traumatic events and undergone formal training in stress debriefing. It was led by a dynamic lady who had decades of experience in hardcore psychotherapy of first responders and was married to a guy on a large PD in the bay area. (I wondered why I had never heard of them when I needed them during all my incidents. I wondered if they cared that I was already living beyond what I could take.)

Word came in that search and rescue had retrieved the guys and that the coroner was about to bring their bodies into a local mortuary. They were looking for guys to go and meet them at the mortuary, either to help ID them or for some other reason. All of us from the station who were not out at the scene went. I remember feeling sick all over my body. I knew in my mind what was going on, but it just did not seem real.

We got to the mortuary and the coroner van backed up and two of our guys from the station got out and came back to us. (I would find out later that these guys spent the time from the scene to the mortuary cleaning our brothers up. They did not want our last memory of them to see them in such a dirty state). The senior guy gave a statement that I wished I had listened to. He said that they looked bad (but didn't say what he and the other guy had done). He said that if there were any among us who were having second thoughts about what we were about to do, that there was no shame in remembering them in life, as they were when we last saw them. Some of the guys did leave. I wished I would have.

The door opened to the van and there was a lot of mud on the floor and two body bags. They needed help pulling the bodies out and then set down onto two gurneys. I don't know how I got there, but I found myself as the first guy up against the van. They slid the first bag and I felt one of the guy's legs fall into my arms. Inside I was screaming, NO!

I wanted to vomit and cry so bad, but I couldn't find the tears.

We were there to receive and identify them so the families wouldn't have to. The scene was horrible, and I can't get it out of my mind. This is almost impossible to write about as it is. I am unable to go there and put it into words. It would not be right. They were heroes who were now in the hands of the Lord.

We went back to the station and the entire division command and peer support team were there. The head therapist did a very good job summarizing the last 24 hours. She told us how difficult the next day's debriefing would be and she was not kidding.

I laid on the floor all night long in front of the TV watching anything for a distraction. My wife went straight to bed. I do not recall any words being said at all.

The next morning came around and I almost did not go in for the debriefing.

It was mandatory. I ended up going in because I was already one of the targets of management and I did not want to be in a worse place than I presently found myself.

The debrief was hours long, but we all sat in a circle with our dispatchers who were on that night. The therapist explained the ground rules. We would go in a circle and talk about the obvious and our feelings, where we were, etc. with no holds barred.

I recall one of the lesser targets, but a target nonetheless, sharing. He had a lot of rage pent up toward management and he let it show. His voice was intense and he wondered out loud why good guys like ours had to die and poor excuses for people like what we had been subjected to, work for, and victims of were allowed to live. This man had at least one, maybe more black belts in martial arts. I believe I heard him express a desire to kill/harm these people with his bare hands.

I wanted to jump up and clap because I felt the same way. I know others in the room did, too. I later told someone on the peer support team that I felt the same way and that the moment they left, management would come for us and the persecution would get worse. The guy just stared at me in stunned disbelief and said nothing. I would not have to wait long to be proven right. I could not sit still in the debrief session. I had to rock back and forth, rubbing my hands on my legs with a trash can in front of me so I had something to throw up in.

When my time finally did come, I just began to spew. I talked about the shift swap, how terrible I felt, and how I wished I could have been in that car instead of them. One of the guys who is a good friend to this day, reminded me in a calm voice that I was not only wishing myself into that car, but my partner as well. He went on to say something that I would later use to frame my whole career.

He said for me to look at it as a sacrifice and do my best not to waste it. Make something from it.

A short time before this incident, our evil commander had been promoted for his wonderful work. We had another who was not much better, but was not an evil man. He had just taken command and did not know most of us very well. He was out just for himself. He heard my confession and decided it would make a great news story. He went out to the many news media outside and gave an update complete with a revelation that an officer had switched shifts the night in question and was now suffering from survivor guilt.

That was an ultimate breach of the confidentiality rules of the debriefing. Too late, the word was out. The media really wanted to talk to the officer. At least he did not give my name.

The day of the memorial service rolled around. I was one of the honor guards at the base of the stage, next to one of the big portraits of the guys. We had to stand perfectly tall and at attention. I recall Ricky's nine- or ten-year-old daughter was so brave she stood up there and sang a solo, standing right behind me. It was God who gave me the strength to stand there. From that moment on, I could not stand to hear little kids sing. When my girls would sing at school functions or church musicals, I hid my tears in the dim lights or got up and stood in the back.

We were off for about two weeks, but eventually had to go back. It seemed each and every citizen group and club did a function or benefit or recognition for the guys' families. Somehow, I was always selected to attend. Some of the guys' family members would also attend. The people behind these functions had the best of intentions, but I relived every moment with each and every function I attended. I cannot imagine how the family members felt.

The Hits Keep on Coming

I was 100 percent right when I told the Peer Support that supervision and command would be coming for some of us, but I didn't know how right I would be. When Peer Support pulled out after the service, that was it. Nothing was left in place for those of us who were struggling.

> **Within a few weeks, the death cloud was back and busy as ever.**

I found myself working the same highway where the guys were killed. It was indescribable the courage it took just to drive by the spot, seeing the big cross and the various items left as a memorial was a big reminder.

I was 40+ miles from the station out Highway 166 just a couple of months after the guys' passing. I received a call just a short way away from where I was, of a head-on collision. I arrived within a couple of minutes, before the three-man fire truck. A mid-sized sedan had hit a pickup truck head-on at a high speed. The sedan driver turned out to be a drug dealer from the county to the north and had enough drugs in his system to drop an elephant. His speedometer was stuck at 80 or 85 MPH. How reliable that was I don't know. The impact was so hard that the belted-in driver of the sedan was moved, still in his seat, to the middle of the front of the car and was unconscious.

The driver of the pickup was an older gentleman with his wife next to him in the passenger seat. Head-on contact had been made from the driver side of one car to the driver side of the pickup truck. There were several motorists who had stopped and were standing there. All of them screaming and shouting, but all were completely unwilling or unable to help me.

I reached inside to get a pulse from the sedan driver, only to find none. I had to move on. The driver of the pickup was a very large athletic man who had to be close to over 300 pounds. His dash had been pushed up almost onto his chest, pinning him against his seat. Both arms were raised above the dash but looked so broken and disfigured they seemed almost like compound fractures. He was extremely pinned in the vehicle. His wife was injured, but not severely.

All I could do was hold C-spine on the pickup driver and try to reassure him and his wife. Somehow, the three-man station of the county fire department materialized in front of me. I do not recall seeing them arrive. The medic was assessing the driver of the sedan. The pickup truck driver kept telling me how much pain he was in and that it was getting really hard to breathe. I knew what was happening.

He said, "I'm gonna die, aren't I? I'm gonna die."

I told him that he was not going to die because this was on my beat and nobody died or did anything on my beat without my permission.

The medic said the driver of the sedan was dead and began assessing the truck driver's wife because they had to get her out in order to get to him. The gentleman kept telling me how it was now very hard to breathe and kept saying he felt like he was dying. I maintained C-spine but leaned into and whispered a heartfelt prayer into the man's ear. A peace seemed to come over him. At that time, the medic relieved me because I had to close the highway because the helicopter was landing.

I was about 50 yards from the crash, holding traffic as the helicopter landed. I was holding traffic when I was advised over the radio that the gentleman had died and his body was left at the scene. I had to start my investigation and had to get his driver's license off his body. I found myself face-to-face with the man I could only try to comfort. I could only stand there for a moment.

The drug dealer's car had hundreds and hundreds of pounds of belongings as well as drugs and scales used in the sale of drugs. It took hours to process the car and sort the evidence. In the meantime, my commander had decided to have our specialty traffic collision team come out and investigate the collision and I would only assist. I was a bit relieved because I was just trying to stay alive from the load I was carrying.

As I was leaving the scene, the sergeant in charge of the team gave me several personal effects of the gentleman and his wife. He told me to take them to their family members who had gathered at the hospital. I did not want to go, but the Lord needed me there as a comfort to the gentleman's son.

I did as I was ordered. The son was extremely distraught. Somehow, I found it inside me to put my arm around him and talk and share the last moments I had with his father. This included our prayer, what we talked about, and how his dad was worried about his mom and his family, and that his parents had done everything right. I could tell I was really reaching this young man and helping him bear the load. It made me feel that I wasn't just there to constantly clean bodies off the road and I was really making a big difference in somebody's life.

Several weeks later, this young man wrote a very touching letter to the editor in the newspaper about our time together. He could not remember my name, but I preferred it that way.

My end-of-the-scene management investigation, processing the evidence, time at the hospital, and booking the evidence at the station amounted to two hours of overtime.

The next day, when I walked into the station, a sergeant that had transferred into our station a year or so before was standing at the end of the hall.

He pointed at me and screamed in a really high-pitched voice like he was demon-possessed, "You! Into the lieutenant's office, now!" He was trembling like he was about to explode.

I walked into the office with the sergeant. The lieutenant commander was sitting at his desk and asked why I had taken so much time on the crash. The sergeant and he then called me a thief because I had stolen two hours of overtime from the people of the state of California. The sergeant was still enraged and was yelling explicative descriptions of his opinion of the situation he had created. The lieutenant's opinion changed when I merely pointed out that I was tasked by the on-scene sergeant to go to the hospital and that had taken over two hours including all the questions the family understandably had. It was not my idea. The lieutenant was visibly changed but would not shut his sergeant up or apologize. I was just dismissed.

More Death

Just a few days later, I found myself working the 101 freeway. My beat allowed me to go home for dinner. I was talking to my mother-in-law who had asked why I seemed to tremble and seemed distraught. She knew of the relentless persecution and had been working on getting me in to see a lawyer. I was telling her about all the death and destruction when another crash call came in on my beat. A vehicle had run into a tree with multiple injuries.

I looked down at the ground and almost started crying as I said, "See, more death!"

I ran out of the house and raced to the scene. As usual, I was the first one to arrive on the scene. It was a large older sedan with several Hispanic youths, ages one-and-a-half to seventeen. The seventeen-year-old was driving. Several people ran up to me and said it was bad and that the girl in the middle front was dead. The fire department arrived, but there were so many major injuries, we all had to perform patient care.

Blood-curdling screams were coming out of the car along with the sounds of the child crying. I noticed that all those riding in the back seat, with the exception of the young child who was in a car seat, had broken femurs (hip bones). The driver looked like the left half of her body had been enveloped by the door. The girl in the middle front looked nearly cut in half and deceased.

Within seconds, a man and woman ran up to me claiming to be the middle-front passenger's parents. Someone had called them and said their daughter was dead. She was only fifteen. The parents were very distraught and wanted to run up to the car. Somehow, I kept them from running up and seeing the horrible scene inside the car. I told them I had not heard that anyone was dead, but I would get someone to talk with them as soon as I knew anything.

They said, "She just can't die. She has a little baby."

My heart sank into my stomach because I knew their daughter was dead.

The extrication of all the occupants took over three-and-a-half hours with the driver still trapped. The medical decision was made to call a surgeon to the scene to amputate the driver's left leg to get her out. The fire department kept trying and was able to free her at the last minute before the surgeon was set up. I thanked God that I did not have to tell the parents of the deceased girl. I did go the extra mile in trying to comfort the family and the families of the driver and the other passengers.

The next two days were a living hell. I could not sleep or eat. I could not concentrate on a single thing for more than a few seconds. I was visibly shaking and fidgeting if I sat, but nobody seemed to notice or care.

Dr. Death

Long before this, I had earned the nickname "Dr. Death." Someone even taped it on my locker. One day at the end of a shift, I walked into the report writing room. There was our shift and the one coming on.

A good friend of mine said in jest, "Ew, there's Dr. Death. Stay back."

We all had a good laugh, but first responders can be very superstitious. I noticed that nobody would come onto my beat for coffee. I pointed that fact out one day to a few of the guys and one of them said, "It's not you. We just don't want to come onto your beat and have the death cloud follow us. You can feel free to meet us on our beat(s)."

I had a more prominent nickname of "Elvis." Several older ladies at different incidents had commented how I looked like a younger Elvis in front of my beat partners. They stuck a small portrait of Elvis on my locker, too.

I knew and understood what they meant by the death cloud. I did not blame them. However, I was already hurting badly and struggling with day-to-day life and that made me feel even lonelier.

Each and every first responder station, office, or yard has a "Dr. Death." Those of you who are first responders know exactly who I am talking about and are probably giggling right now. It is somebody who death has just glommed onto and won't let go. The cloud can shift from one to another. It's just a very strange fact in "first responderville."

About three days after this collision, I was driving into the station to start my shift. I saw the parents of the dead girl with about 8-10 other people standing outside with my commander. They left just as I pulled into the back parking lot. I walked into the building and was brought into the commander's office by my sergeant (the one who seemed like he had a heart in the ER the day of the multi-fatality accident).

I sat down facing the commander with the sergeant standing next to him. They handed me a plant and said that the families of the kids in the crash were just here and they wanted to thank me for showing so much compassion and care at the scene. The commander and the sergeant then asked if I was really that nice and if I

had told the newspaper reporter that they seemed like a group of good kids out driving. I said I had shown them compassion given the gravity of the situation. I added that I had not worded my statement exactly as it was quoted.

The commander launched into a statement that showing that much kindness was "pretty unprofessional." He went on further, "That girl who died had a baby out of wedlock."

It was then implied that I was helping the wrong people.

He then said, "We think you need to find another line of work."

I felt a huge wellspring of emotion welling up inside of me. Rage, sadness, hate, and despair. I told them nobody wished they were in a different line of work more than I did at that moment. I said I was struggling with basic survival and wished I were dead and would never forgive myself for trading shifts with the guys and getting them killed. I barely got that out and burst into tears. I could see the sergeant felt bad and was near tears himself, but the commander obviously could have cared less. He just piled it on how I could go do something else and that there was no shame in it. I actually went right back out to my beat!

Can you imagine trying to function, let alone drive a police cruiser and try to do the job in that frame of mind? When you and a few others are relentlessly singled out and picked on by management because you are kind or maybe have the wrong last name, you tend to make mistakes. Don't get me wrong. I made them and I owned what I said and did. Even the sergeant who seemed tasked with driving me out, said "You have never lied to me. I will give you that."

By the next day, I was truly unable to function. It had all caught up with me. I could not go any farther. I don't even remember going to the doctor, but when he heard what had been happening, he took me off duty on stress. The state compensation paperwork needed a reason for the leave. I summarized all the events and wrote, "Even my commander said I need to find another line of work."

I would find out years later that what I wrote caught the eyes of upper management who knew what had been going on at our station for years and did nothing. However, this was so over the top and my story was gaining so much local interdepartmental publicity, they had to do something. They told the commander that his career was over and to not bother attempting to promote any higher.

Guide to Surviving in the Line of Duty

At the end of each chapter, I will share suggestions to help you deal with the emotional roller coaster after experiencing trauma or tragedy in your own personal line of duty.

I was experiencing survivor guilt. I blamed myself for changing shifts with these other two officers. No matter what your trauma or tragedy, our natural tendency is to blame ourselves thinking there was something else we should have done or in some way caused it.

Does this describe how you are experiencing "survivor guilt?

Our peer support unit showed up. It was the first I had ever heard of this group. It was a group of uniformed and non-uniformed people from the department who had been involved in traumatic events and undergone formal training in stress debriefing.

Who is helping you carry these emotional burdens?

Read John 15:13.

One of the guys who is a good friend to this day, said for me to look at it as a sacrifice and do my best not to waste it. Make something from it.

I also believe God has sent this man to help me through the dark times.

Ask God to send you a friend to help you through your dark times and He will because He loves you.

Chapter 3

LIFE ON THE RUBBER GUN SQUAD AND WANDERING IN THE WILDERNESS

AS FUNNY AS IT MAY SOUND, THE RUBBER GUN squad is where you really land if you are off duty on stress leave for any reason in law enforcement. They take your gun, your badge, and you must sign a paper removing your peace officer powers. For many of us, this is the final straw. Who we are is entirely wrapped up in that badge. This is how the system starts. It is supposed to help, but instead shoves you over the edge if the injury has not done that yet. Many suicides occur at this point because the one last thing you have left is gone.

For some unknown or unwritten reason, your coworkers now cannot have anything to do with you. I associated it with the lions coming for the gazelles. When the rear gazelle gets tired or hurt, the lions close in on it and the herd goes running off in the opposite direction while the lions feed. Going out on stress is viewed as a weakness. They don't want to be associated with it or they don't want the cloud following them. I just remember being so lonely for the guys I worked with that I would rush to my front door every time I heard squeaky brakes outside.

(Police car brakes always squeak). I only recall two of the guys coming by the house, once each, in four-and-a-half years.

Workman's Comp

If the stress of the injury you go out on does not shove you over the edge, the workman's comp process will.

I had to go to so many different doctors and appointments that they were impossible to keep straight. Some of the therapists I was sent to would start crying or tears come down their faces. You know you are really messed up when your stories make doctors and therapists cry.

What was up for discussion was if I was going to retire on a psych disability or be off for a period of time not to exceed one year. I had to relive all the events I have written about here and much more, numerous times. I had to relive it with each new doctor or each session about walking hand-in-hand with death, having it follow me for years, and the ceaseless persecution from some supervision and management.

My body was breaking down now, also. I was diagnosed with Crohn's disease, Colitis, high blood pressure, Meiners disease (I had to be taken to the ER on duty because of severe dizziness and violent vomiting), atrial fibrillation, years of ceaseless ringing and roaring in my ears (the roaring would fluctuate with my heartbeat), and severe lower back pain. I was only thirty-three.

Being off meant I had all day and all night to dwell on my situation and overwhelm myself. One of the few things I did right was that I never stopped going to the gym five days a week. I also kept going to church. My wife was of a different faith, but worked on Sundays anyway, so I always went alone and took my two-year-old little girl. I would drop her off at the children's church and go into the main service and sit alone.

PTSD was not a term yet, but I had all the signs, on steroids! I could not enter the church through the front and talk to the greeters. Instead, I found a side entrance that had a janitor's closet with a restroom in it. It was only a few yards to the side doors to the sanctuary where I would sit on the very end of the pew three steps from the door. Within moments of people arriving, I would start to sweat profusely. While standing, I would feel numerous drops of sweat run down my back, to the point my shirt would stick to my back and people would stare. My heart would beat so hard, I could feel my pulse behind my eyes. This would happen in any crowded place I was in. This went on for over twenty years.

I could not escape it in my sleep. My dreams were very vivid and sometimes violent. Many times, I would dream I was working graveyard shifts with one of my deceased friends. It seemed we would work an entire shift together, but they looked exactly how they did at the mortuary. At or near the end of the shift, I would get the courage to reach over and touch them and every time they were ice cold, they would disappear. To this day, I wake up, literally wet from sweat, having soaked my shirt. My wife would say that it was only because I was overweight. This sort of puts a perspective of what my relationship was like with her. (I will attempt to go more into detail later)

The only thing I really had at home was my little girl. I took her everywhere I went and we had a daily routine we followed. I lived day-to-day and this is the only thing in my mind that was worth getting up for in the morning. I would read my Bible and pray, but most of the time, I could only keep praying, "God please help me, please help me, please help me" over and over. They were the only words I had for a very long time. He knew what I needed.

> **If God, help me are all you have, don't stop! If those are the only words you can muster, keep saying them. He will come through.**

From my point of view, my relationship with my wife was fairly non-existent. Praying or reading the Bible together usually ended up in fights. I remember entire anniversaries and holidays spent fighting. I felt she did not understand and what's more, didn't really care. I remember at some point in all this, sitting on my couch with tears streaming down my face. My wife was sitting across the room flipping through a magazine. She stopped and looked right at me and went back to flipping through her magazine.

Our little girl saw this, walked over and put her hands on my knee, and said, "It's okay daddy, I'm here."

As first responders, in my case, law enforcement, we are a very closed society. Nobody knows what we go through. Nobody has the slightest idea of what it's like to have to put the body parts of a child in a bag and an hour later go home for dinner and try to listen to your spouse air their grievances with you.

What we don't realize is how much we isolate. We isolate either to protect our families, or because we know they will never understand, or we just do not want to re-live things again. Even as I thought about my wife, I wondered why she didn't care. What I didn't see were the many ways I would drive her away and keep her away.

We had been arguing for several days and my wife went to her mother's house for a few days, but had said things were pretty much over. I was awakened the next morning at 2 A.M. with my heart going like a trip hammer. It felt like I was riding down a roller coaster that did not stop. I had this feeling before when I was stressed at work. I tried getting up, but found I could hardly stand and nearly passed out. There was nobody home but me. I managed to get it together enough to drive the 2 miles to the hospital.

I remember walking up to the ER and telling the ward clerk that I may have the flu. I just felt weird. They took me back to a room and the nurse hooked me up to a cardiac monitor. She blinked really hard three or four times and ran to the back of the ER, woke up the doctor who came running into my room, wiping his eyes. The nurse came in behind him with the crash cart and switched on the defibrillator, warming up the paddles. The doctor told me I was in atrial fibrillation and was in danger of having a stroke if they could not get me back into sinus rhythm.

I felt helpless. All I could think about was my buddies who died. I was almost angry that it wasn't me. I knew this meant more and more medication for probably the rest of my life, but what I did not know was that I would become close friends with the defibrillator, and it would ultimately land me on the operating table at Stanford.

What do you do when everything around you is crashing down, and you are not allowed to leave the county unless you notify the very people who had a big hand in landing you where you are?

Intrusive Thoughts and Triggers

Yes, I tried filling my time with my daughter, but there's another ugly aspect of PTSD called "intrusive thoughts" and "triggers." I would be playing with her and if she started crying or got hurt and began screaming, I found I would have images or flashbacks of a variety of horrific scenes involving children from the job. It was not like Hollywood shows where a flashback is like going unconscious and teleporting back in time. I could actually see and hear these children suffering pain and agony while watching or helping my own child. They did tune everything out in my periphery for a short time. They were usually very short, but enough to jam up my heart rate, nauseate me, and cause me to sweat profusely.

Likewise with sirens. I could be in the middle of a conversation and a siren would start sounding. I would actually abruptly stop and try to refocus on the conversation, but all I could see was myself in the driver's seat of one of our 5.0 Mustang patrol cars in pursuit, shifting gears, and talking on the radio. This happens to this very day. This happened on several occasions while I was in the middle of therapy sessions. Each time, the therapist picked up on it. Sometimes, I would lose my train of thought and forget what I was talking about, or I would visibly struggle to stay on track until the siren stopped or got so far away, I couldn't hear it anymore.

Even trying to sleep during this time was a challenge. With nothing but time on my hands, I thought about my circumstances, all of my past events, and a bleak future.

This would also spawn nightmares and full-on flashbacks of all kinds. I wanted so badly to have been the one, like I should have been, in my buddies' car, that I had a recurring dream that I was in it, driving on Highway 166 to the point they plunged into the river. Just before plunging in, I would see my wife and daughter standing on the shoulder looking at me, over and over. If it ever took a break, it was some other job-related nightmare centered around death, suffering, or past scenes of supervision or management.

More medication, sleeping pills, triple doses of Nexium, just to barely ease my stomach trouble, not to mention all the other medication I was taking. I had nothing but time on my hands. That was my normal day. Oddly, I was not on any psych meds. It was amazing how many people were full of advice, but were not willing to sit and talk with me. The thing I heard the most about the guys was, "It was their time, it's not your fault." Not having someone who had experienced what I had and able to know where I really was, made things worse. They all meant well, but it did nothing to ease things.

Somebody told me not to feel so guilty about the guys. I heard myself say, "I no longer feel guilty, I feel responsible." When I heard that, I knew I had crossed a line into an area few if any ever returned.

I was also feeling more pressure from work about a return date and would actually feel like throwing up after each month's fake token, "How are ya doin', We're here for ya." I finally listened to someone and got an attorney just to stop having to talk to supervision and management. It was the right move, but with the very wrong attorney. I was very thorough and told him all that had happened, including a blow-by-blow of the awful things management had done. He was only interested in getting me retired, medically. Oddly, he ignored and never spoke to the things about management.

He told me, "I can settle your case over a game of golf."

He was a former CHP officer and I felt he, of all people, could empathize. I would call with updates on my case and at the end of the call, I felt like I was really bothering them.

I called one time and got the attorney's assistant who said, "Are we even representing you?" She could not find anything about my case.

After nearly a year, my mother-in-law (a family law attorney) took me to the #1 work comp attorney in the state who sat and listened very intently. What I had to say even shocked him. He shook his head and said he really could not help me now with my comp case. My case was only worth a very small amount and he even showed me in a book on a graph how things would go. However, he said I had a very big case for a malpractice suit against my attorney and he offered to sue him for me. (My other attorney had bragged that he had a different colored Rolls Royce for each day of the week.)

This new attorney advised me that mine had let a lot of labor law violations go and ignored many other legally actionable things, including violations of the Peace Officers Bill of Rights. Those who violate it have to pay personally, not the department. However, he advised me that my attorney had let things go so long, that statute had passed for me to get relief through the court system. All I had was a beautiful case of malpractice now.

By this time, I was such a mess and so furious that I knew I could not make it through endless court proceedings, so I just dropped that idea and my old attorney. I would later find out that my attorney was "in bed" with the department and did not want to take on anything that would discredit it. In the coming years, I would also watch as other coworkers who worked with me and for me were let down or screwed over time and time again by this same attorney despite my personal story. Two of them came to me to get my full story and any advice to sue him for malpractice.

It's really hard to be at your lowest ebb and the person you think is fighting for you actually does not care at all and whose only interest is to get you in and out quickly while keeping any bad news about the department quiet. It was a letdown and a lonely feeling I will never forget.

I am unable to remember how many doctors I saw. I had my own medical doctor, my own psychologist, the state had its own doctor and psychiatrist, and I now had to go to a neutral psychologist or psychiatrist. He was to decide my fate.

He was one of the deans of psychology or psychiatry at USC or UCLA. He was an extremely nice and caring doctor. I felt totally at ease talking to him. It was supposed to be a two-hour appointment but went well over three hours. I was his last appointment of the day and I went so long that I noticed the building's lights and air conditioning had shut off.

I found myself, white-knuckled, clutching one of the pillows on the couch. At the end of the appointment, he said, "I don't know why you are not in a rubber room. Have you ever heard of the term battle fatigue? You've got it **bad**!"

He told me I was pretty much finished/retired as of that moment or as fast as he could get the paperwork in. In a way, I was relieved, knowing I would never have to go back into the non-stop death and persecution.

Another form of suffering is the hurry up and wait. I occupied my time as best I could, but weeks and months would go by with no answers to anything.

The last shoe finally dropped on September 30, 1999. I was unceremoniously notified through the mail that I was finally retired. In the same letter, they told me I could never again carry a concealed weapon. They wanted my ID card and said to report to the nearest CHP office for a fresh picture for my "Rubber Gun Squad Retirement Card."

It had finally sunk in, I was done. The last remaining bit of who I was and my whole identity was in that badge. I had to turn that in also. When I got it back, the gold ribbon across the top said, "RETIRED" not "HONORABLY RETIRED." That put it into perspective that even my honor was gone. I really didn't think I could feel worse, but this helped. The officers at the station asked if I would like a retirement party and I said no. Though they meant well, they could not understand, there was nothing to celebrate. I also did not want to have to ever see two of the sergeants or the commander ever again and they would be there.

By this time, I had already been off for a year. Now what? I had initially gone to college to teach school and with my small settlement, I finished my degree and got a teaching credential. However, there was a huge teacher glut and all I could get was substitute spots that paid $80/day before tax. My small pension was $2,400 a month. My wife was a registered nurse. We pretty much lived hand to mouth, but our bills were more than we made and soon we were using credit cards for shortfalls.

We began to sell stuff. We had to sell our bedroom furniture and were down to sleeping on the floor on a box spring and mattress. Our little girl had some bedroom furniture, we had a couch and a coffee table, but not much more. There was nothing in our room.

The next three-and-a-half years were terrible, with the exception of one small bright light. I occupied the time the best I could, but I was constantly reminded of the past, especially the deaths of the guys. Day and night, the full effects of PTSD ran rampant. My wife and I drifted further and further apart, as if it could have been any worse. I never took a drink and was not taking any psych meds. I felt that at least I faced my troubles sober and head-on, but I was just running. I stayed in church, desperate for a miracle, but still avoiding people and unable to pray much.

Ministering to Others

> **One Sunday, the pastor taught that "through ministering to others, you are ministered to."**

I had been long-term substitute teaching and found it was almost as bad as working the streets. I then figured out that I would rather be shot at than teach full-time, but I needed a full-time job. I began looking out of state, but job markets had tightened up since 9/11.

I had been looking in North Carolina at state park jobs and found several I would like. However, in praying about it, the Lord kept bringing the fact that through ministering to others, you are ministered to. I could not shake it. Believe me, I tried because I knew where that was going to go.

I felt the Lord leading me back to the CHP. All my doctors and therapists had told me that I could never go back to law enforcement. I had been through way too much. Nobody had ever come back from this far out on the rubber gun squad. I pointed that out to the Lord.

> **I've never heard voices, but I felt a message come through that was so loud and clear, "I didn't ask if you could take it. There are people who need Me and are going to need you because of what I have brought you through. They need to hear your message about Me. Do not worry, I will be with you, I will give you the strength and the words."**

At first, I really questioned it. How could I go back to something that did so much damage to me physically and mentally? I still could not get over the mountain that stood in front of me of the major guilt over the deaths of the guys.

How could someone as bad as me have anything at all to offer anyone?

How much nerve would I ever have showing my face in a CHP station ever again?

Suddenly, the words of one of my close friends in the station came through very loud. It was during our stress debriefing. I was melting down and spilling everything about the shift swap, wishing out loud that I would have been in that car.

He said, "Dan, look at it as a sacrifice. They did for you what you would have done for them."

As soon as that came back to me, I felt another jolt that said, "Now, do something with it!"

Immediately, the idea hit me that I was going to see those guys again, someday. What better thing to do than to show them what I did with their sacrifice? By going back into the mess and help pull others out of where I had been and helping to save lives and families, I would be making the utmost of what they did for me that night so long ago.

BAM! Instant motivation. Not to say that I was not scared or apprehensive. Everywhere I went throughout the reinstatement process, people looked at me funny. Nobody had ever come back from this or something this bad. The reinstatement process was even harder than the process when I was initially hired. I had to go to three sets of doctors: my medical doctor and therapist, the state's medical doctor and therapist, and a neutral medical doctor and therapist. Another whole year and more of "hurry up and wait."

Meanwhile, a previous CHP commissioner had ended our chaplain program because he did "not want a lawsuit on his hands." We had eighteen suicides within twenty-one months. I know of a couple more who did it after resigning or termination and were not included in this. Was the removal of our chaplains the sole cause for this? Probably not, but it just made it all the harder to talk to someone. One of those who suicided at his home was not missed or his body found for two full weeks after. Yes, he had driven his friends and family away, but nobody thought to check on him.

First Responders:

How often do we automatically distance ourselves from those of us who are struggling, whether it is their fault or not?

Do we see them as unclean? Weak? Will we catch it if we get too close?

Or is it that we just don't want to invest too much of ourselves?

Is it because we just don't want to get too close because then we may end up actually caring?

Take it from someone who was desperate for contact from those he served with: no effort is too small or wasted. A call, a card, a text, anything!

> "God comforts us *so that* we can comfort others.
>
> God grants us mercy *so that* we can be merciful to others.
>
> God stands whole-heartedly with us in our suffering *so that* we will stand whole-heartedly with others who are suffering.
>
> God never leaves us alone in our suffering *so that* we won't leave others alone in theirs." – Pastor Dave Zuleger[1]

Guide to Surviving in the Line of Duty

At the end of each chapter, I will share suggestions to help you deal with the emotional roller coaster after

---

[1] www.desiringgod.org

experiencing trauma or tragedy in your own personal line of duty.

We tend to isolate ourselves either to protect our families, or we think they will never understand, or we just do not want to re-live things again.

Do you find yourself isolated from others and try to handle your emotional roller coaster on your own?

One of the few things I did right during this time was that I never stopped going to the gym five days a week. I also kept going to church. I would read my Bible and pray, but most of the time, I could only keep praying, "God please help me, please help me, please help me" over and over.

If that's all you have, don't stop! If those are the only words you can muster, keep saying them. God will come through.

Read Hebrews 13:5.

I believe God keeps His promises.

How could someone as bad as me have anything at all to offer anyone?

Read 2 Corinthians 1:3-4.

The Lord kept bringing the fact that through ministering to others, you are ministered to. **I've never heard voices, but I felt a message come through that was so loud and clear, "I didn't ask if you could take it. There are people who need Me and are going to need you because of what I have brought you through. They need to hear your message about Me. Do not worry, I will be with you, I will give you the strength and the words."**

My friend had said, "Dan, look at it as a sacrifice. They did for you what you would have done for them."

As soon as that came back to me, I felt another jolt that said, "Now, do something with it!"

By going back into the mess and help pull others out of where I had been and helping to save lives and families, I would be making the utmost of what they did for me that night so long ago.

Pray and ask God how you can use what you've been through to help pull others out and help save lives and families?

God comforts us so that we can comfort others.

God grants us mercy so that we can be merciful to others.

God stands whole-heartedly with us in our suffering so that we will stand whole-heartedly with others who are suffering.

God never leaves us alone in our suffering so that we won't leave others alone in theirs.

Chapter 4

REINSTATEMENT, EYE OF THE TIGER

"Eye Of The Tiger"
Rising up, back on the street. Did my time, took my chances.
Went the distance, now I'm back on my feet.
Just a man and his will to survive.
So many times it happens too fast.
You trade your passion for glory.
Don't lose your grip on the dreams of the past.[2]

THE ROAD BACK WAS FRAUGHT WITH MASSIVE potholes and obstacles. Delays, reports, appointments, you name it. The biggest one came the night before I had my physical agility test at the CHP Academy in West Sacramento. I drove the seven hours from my

---

[2] Reference: Survivor - Eye Of The Tiger Lyrics | AZLyrics.com from movie Rocky May 29, 1982

home, stayed in a hotel, and had dinner with a friend who was a Placer County Sheriff's deputy. I was already very nervous and went back to my room to get to sleep early for the test.

Around 1 A.M. I woke in sustained atrial fibrillation again. I could barely stand. It felt like I was on a never-ending roller coaster, going straight down. I remember praying to ask God to help me and asking Him why He would bring me this far only to be disqualified because I couldn't even stand up. I called my parents for prayer and I just kept praying, "God help me, God help me." I did not call my wife because we were just not getting along and anything in the realm of religion usually ended us up in a fight.

Normally, I would have needed to be admitted to the hospital, sedated, and defibrillated to get the heart back to sinus rhythm and keep me from having a stroke. Around 4:30 A.M., as fast as it came, it left. I was tired from being up all night, but I was good enough to pass the test. The officer administering the test had heard of me or what I was re-instating from. I was able to tell him just a little about how I made it and what I felt the Lord was doing. He shared how the Lord had richly blessed him and saved his marriage. It was highly encouraging to hear. From this point on, I would run into many people who had heard of me or my story, and almost every time, it was as an instant foot in the door.

Reinstatement, Eye of the Tiger

It was a good feeling being sworn back in. I felt as if I had returned home after a long trip. While attending reinstatement, two high-ranking chiefs from the commissioner's office came and visited with me. They personally apologized for the hell my supervision and management had put me through for all those years in Santa Maria. I was stunned but deeply touched. They said they were not perfect but they were trying to change things for the better. That went a long way with me. I was very grateful. The seven-week reinstatement went fast and I found myself going to the Santa Barbara station to work the road. Unlike when and where I left, I now found myself the senior afternoon shift car geek.

I was very apprehensive that I would land right back into the same supervision/management nightmare I had before. It was a huge answer to prayer to find that it was a great group of folks from the top down, uniformed and non-uniformed. I actually felt joy again doing my job and helping those who were in need.

Not long after starting over, I received a message that someone from the Peer Support Unit wanted to talk to me and they were coming down from HQ in Sacramento to interview me. I was excited to hear that our commissioner had not only taken the first responder suicide epidemic seriously, but to heart. He knew from experience what we faced out there and saw the need instead of an impending lawsuit. He restored the Chaplain program and greatly expanded the Peer

Support Unit. When I retired, they were just helpers who had been through traumatic events. They truly did care but once the debrief ended, they and the therapist were gone with little, if any follow-up.

Those in the Employee Assistance Unit, the commissioner at the time, and our departmental therapist, Beth Dansi, took the mission to a whole new level. In order to be a peer, you had to be interviewed and been through some real deep water. You were then sent through a very rough two-week initial training in the Mitchell Method of Stress Debriefing. There were constant week-long updates and yearly meetings to assess where we were.

Once we were up and running, our names and personal phone numbers were on a list that was posted in each CHP station statewide for calls at any hour of the day or night for anyone uniformed or non-uniformed who may be struggling or may have just experienced a traumatic event.

We would also roll to specific stations for line-of-duty deaths, coworker suicides, set up for stress debriefings, be there to assist the personnel affected, and get a lay of the land for the responding therapist. However, our main goal was to be there for those affected by whatever the emergency.

My interview came and I was quite flattered that they would send two people from Sacramento to interview me. One was uniformed, the other non. They were heavy hitters in the trauma department. I would learn they were two of the main coordinators. They told me they had heard about my story and wanted to hear a little more.

After taking them down my road, I noticed they were both crying, and I wasn't close to being done. I noticed they were also very angry at the level of departmental betrayal that was woven in my entire story. At the end of it all, they were also amazed I wasn't in a rubber room. They asked if I would like to be a part of Peer Support and I jumped at the chance.

I knew the Lord was in this. I had not sought this out. They came to me.

Initial training was held at the academy in Sacramento. I was not ready for it. I went in thinking it would be just a matter of learning the methodology of a debriefing. I was also not ready for it spiritually with the Lord. I still had not spent the time I needed in prayer for God's help and guidance in what was to come.

I arrived to find a whole lot of other thoroughly screwed up people there also. We spent what seemed like forever listening to each other's awful experiences and reliving our own, over and over as a class and in groups. You could pretty much tell who was the most screwed up by the number of sighs you heard and how many others you made cry. I rang the bell on both and had to be stopped even though I had so much more to say. I had the perfect blend of trauma and departmental abandonment.

As I have said before, for years it constantly felt like I had a huge lump in my throat. It was so bad, I even had it scoped twice. I had non-stop roaring/ringing in my ears and I could feel my pulse behind my eyes. These two weeks put all that on steroids. I felt ten times worse. It started to improve slightly when we got into the methodology/nuts and bolts of debriefings until one particular PowerPoint slide.

The therapist was talking about how sideways our debrief went in Santa Maria and how the commander went out and told the news media everything that had happened in the session and how one officer was suffering from survivor guilt. It included a picture of the guys' car after it was pulled out of the river that I had never seen before. No part of the car was much taller than my knee. I used to go to the wrecking yard and just stand there and stare at it until they finally took it away, but I never saw it next to the river and I had no idea a picture was coming.

I suddenly physically heaved. All the air came out of my body and a very dark pall came over me as if I had just been covered by a large black sheet. My head hit the desk and I began to cry uncontrollably. I think I had to be assisted out of the room. It took longer than I thought to get composed and go back in. (That picture was a huge trigger for me.)

I ended up learning a lot in those two weeks, but I was in no shape to help anyone else anytime soon. I was still required to go to therapy and I still went to church, but I was still too much of a mess to be active in the Peer Support Program. All the way home from Sacramento, all I felt was anger. I was brimming over with anger. I was angry at the department for doing this to me, angry at being such a mess and not feeling the least bit recovered, and angry at my family in advance for not understanding and not caring based on how much empathy I had received up to now.

I arrived home and walked up the sidewalk to the front door. I could tell preparations were underway for a weekend party for my (second) baby daughter's baptism party the next day. I knew in advance of the party, but all I wanted to do was rest in a quiet room or on the couch. I was mentally and physically exhausted.

I walked in the door. Nobody said hello or welcome home. There was no greeting of any kind. Instead, my mother-in-law walked up to me with a forced catty smile and handed me the vacuum cleaner while I was still pulling my suitcase in one hand and holding a jacket in the other. I felt a massive wave of rage (not toward her, believe it or not) come over me to the point where I began to shake and tremble uncontrollably. I threw my things on the floor, grabbed the vacuum out of my mother-in-law's hands, and began running to the door. Our door had a large window that took up the top half of the door. I raised the vacuum and planned to throw it out the window, grab my suitcase, leave, and never come back.

I think I scared her because the next thing I knew, my wife was standing next to me, chewing me out, telling me how hard she and her parents had worked so I could go have fun in Sacramento. I began yelling at her about what I had experienced the last several days and what it had done to me. It was as I had it figured. Nobody cared and nobody could possibly understand.

> **What I was witnessing was a byproduct of self-isolation.**
>
> **How could my wife know what I was going through when I wouldn't say anything?**

I had long ago kissed her off as not caring and unable to even possibly understand. I had isolated so much she did not know or understand what I was going through. I did not realize it, but I was so turned inward that I had convinced myself that she did not care or understand. Any attempt she made I would genuinely see as an attempt to blame or fault me for whatever was happening. Some of our worst fights were over this for years. Luckily, I was not needed in the peer capacity for quite a while.

Settling In

I know what you're thinking. How could any sane, rational person get out of such a long career full of trauma, recover, and even remotely want to go back? All I can say is that the Lord most certainly works in mysterious ways. His plans for us are great and mighty. If we only yield ourselves to Him and let Him have control, He will take what was trash and to our detriment and turn it into gold for our good and His good.

It is a massive beacon to those around us, especially those who knew and worked with us before and saw all we went through, and even witnessed our mistakes, failures, and transgressions. It is the best testimony to redemption from God.

> *"I waited patiently for the Lord* (sometimes waiting is suffering). *He turned to me and heard my cry* (notice the word "turned." Maybe His back was turned on us because we wandered off?). *He lifted me out of the slimy pit, out of the mud and mire; he set my feet on a rock and **gave me a firm place to stand**. He put a new song*

in my mouth, a hymn of praise to our God."
(Psalm 40:1-2 NIV emphasis added)

I began to settle into the Santa Barbara office: the firm place to stand. I began to experience real joy in my life from having wonderful people in my supervision/command structure and being able to not enforce laws, but to actually serve the community and look out for folks and help those in need.

I loved the swing shift. My beat was nothing but ranchland bordered by the Pacific Ocean. Each and every evening, I was blessed to have the choice of seven or eight different beaches to watch the sunset. The entire time, I was thanking God for what He had brought me through. I prayed He would use me for His kingdom and just show me what His plan was for my life from here. He put a new song in my heart and mouth, a hymn of praise to our God.

It was not long before the death cloud resumed where it had left off. I had been dreading it, but somehow knew it would find me again. I began to experience some small but glaring signs that the trauma was affecting my mind in small ways.

I was working my usual ocean-front beat and an elderly couple rolled their car a quarter-mile in front of me, coming to rest upside down. The gentleman, the driver was obviously deceased. I attempted to put it out over the air, but I suddenly could not remember where I was. I had put the first part out, but the most important part, the location, I couldn't say because I actually did not know, even though I really did know. It just was not coming to me.

I could hear my sergeant and the guy on the next beat calling me, repeatedly, over and over on the air for my location. It seemed like forever, but it was only about 15-20 seconds (an eternity in this business). I knew the offramp about two miles to the north, so I put that out and that I was south of that. That was correct, but in this business, it was far too vague. I started first aid on the driver's wife and kept her from looking over to her left until the paramedics got there.

When my sergeant arrived, I could tell he was upset. However, because he spent years on the streets and more importantly, he gave a darn, he could immediately tell I had a hiccup from seeing my first gore in four-and-a-half years.

In the following days, I had plenty of doubts. I asked God, "Why did You bring me back to this? If this is going to keep happening, I won't be any good to anybody." These doubts and fears kept dominating my mind over and over for a good long time. Bottom line, the Lord made it clear that there were no guarantees except those from Him. I needed to learn to rely on Him constantly, not just moment to moment.

Dodging More Bullets

Pursuits, bloody accidents, and critical incidents kept coming, but the Lord made His presence abundantly clear.

This part of the country is known for many things, particularly our wildfire season. My first fire season back was one for the record books. I recall working my beautiful coastal beat when a report of a fire on our north end came in. It was extremely mountainous with sheer peaks and cliffs that ran all along the freeway. In an area near Gaviota Beach, the 101 freeway takes a wicked curve to the north, going through a tunnel in the coastal mountains.

It is a very narrow pass that funnels any kind of breeze into 50-60+ MPH winds. It has tipped over trucks and in one storm, blew a train completely off the tracks. As my luck would have it, this was the exact location of the fire. They produce pillars of smoke that can rise to over 30,000 feet and create their own weather! I have seen lighting and thunderstorms come out of some large smoke plumes in the past.

The fire was moving at an astounding rate and the 101 freeway was closed. I was positioned at the Gaviota Beach entrance, which also was the entrance to a large group of very high-end luxury ranch estates. It was also a radio dead spot, so I could not get messages out to dispatch very easily. I had two other units with me who had to leave to cover other locations. Before they left, we could see one of the massive smoke plumes over the ridge from our location, but it looked as though it was moving our way and we were talking about it. I noticed the younger guy stared at me for a bit. I knew he was thinking that I may not make it if I stayed here.

No sooner had they left than the fire caused a boulder the size of a house to roll down the mountain and block the tunnel for my northbound escape route. Within moments of that happening, several very large eucalyptus trees fell across the southbound lanes blocking my southerly escape. My only escape option was to drive out and onto the beach.

Suddenly, I saw numerous small wild animals running across the freeway passed me, heading toward the beach. I looked straight up and at the top of the ridge, approximately half a mile away and several hundred feet up and I saw a cyclone of fire. It was coming right at me, down the hill at what seemed like over 30 MPH. I had just enough time to turn to my right and run back to my patrol car when I felt intense heat on my back through my Kevlar vest and heard a roar. I looked up toward my patrol car and saw the fire had caught me. It had jumped the freeway and was already burning behind my car. There was now no place to go. The road to the beach was surrounded by 15-20-foot-deep brush. The fire burned all the way down to the beach.

It was very hot and smokey. I made it back to the car and turned on the a/c to recirculate. It was a very nervous next hour or so. I could hear dispatch trying to raise me. I tried replying but they could not copy anything. They put it out to the other units that they had lost contact with me. I could tell from the other units, traffic that there was no way to access my location because of the downed boulder and burning trees across the freeway. I suddenly got the weird feeling like this is what it's like to be missing.

You can bet I prayed hard to the Lord. He gave me a peace and a confidence that He was there and He was always taking care of me. I kept an eagle eye on my patrol car's temperature gauge and noticed that despite the hot summer day and the fact that there was fire on all sides of me, the engine temperature did not rise. I was afraid the heat and smoke would choke out the engine. The Lord's hand was once again on me. It was a very long hour, but when things burned down around me enough, I was able to drive a short distance and contact dispatch that I was okay.

About a week later, the unpredictability of our Santa Ana and Sundowner winds made that same fire very unpredictable which was complicated by the steep terrain. I had just started my shift a few miles south of my earlier incident. I had been talking to an old line-crew foreman who was covered with dirt and soot. He was worried because of the volatility of the fire. He said, "This is the kind of fire we lose people on."

That really stuck with me because a decision had been made the day before to open the freeway in both directions. I remember before leaving the station, telling the sergeant and anyone who would listen that I did not like the way the fire had been moving and to please reconsider and at least shut northbound down. That was also the first thing I told my lieutenant or sergeant when I arrived at my post on the northbound part of the freeway just south of where I had been just a few days prior.

I was even more convinced the longer I stood there waving traffic through to keep going and stop staring at the fire equipment. Traffic had slowed to a virtual crawl and became stop and go. Soon, I had nowhere to wave traffic to. Suddenly, there was another wind shift and a huge increase in smoke. I remember having difficulty breathing and almost vomited. The same old crew-line foreman came running down the dirt road adjacent to the freeway lanes.

His hands were up to his mouth and he was yelling, "The fire is 30 seconds from the freeway! It's headed this way!"

I only had time to get a single radio transmission out that the freeway was grid-locked and the fire was just seconds from the lanes. I also put out on the radio to shut the northbound down and send vehicles southbound, through the center divider if we had to. I could hardly see northbound traffic any more. I ran up to the vehicles and began waving them through the center divider, turning them around, southbound. I could barely breathe, but I had a large number of cars to get out of the area and only seconds to do it. I had no idea if anybody heard my transmission. I had a brand-new officer on the beat south of me and I was wondering if he was close enough to have acted immediately. As it turned out, he was and he was able to get traffic turned around, but it didn't matter. We had far too much stopped traffic to get turned around to make a difference in time.

I watched as the flames roared down the hill into the gully next to the northbound lanes and right back up the other side. I saw numerous vehicles at a stop and saw the faces of a family in one car looking terrified along with the people in the car directly next to them. The flames were literally 15 feet high and made a loud roar. It looked to me like the wind blew the flames fully across both lanes, enveloping all of the cars that were stopped. I thought I was witnessing a mass casualty incident of the worst kind happening right in front of me.

Suddenly, I heard a loud whoop, whoop, whoop, sound. I saw the smoke stop rising and go out to the side. As the smoke parted, I saw one of those huge very old Sikorsky helicopters with one of those large bags of ocean water, let loose on the flames and the vehicles. Right behind them was another helicopter with water and another, dowsing the flames and saving an untold number of lives.

In my humble opinion, every single pilot/crewperson of those birds deserved a Medal of Valor award. To have to fly so close and act so fast took untold courage. They had to have seen disaster coming and acted unilaterally because there was no time to get orders. I believe all those motorists and myself are only alive through their bravery and quick action.

On a side note: If I have the honor of having anyone in first responder management or a leadership role reading this, I respectfully implore you to listen to your field troops. Especially the veteran ones. I could tell I was being ignored by my command staff about keeping the freeway closed. They weren't even listening most likely because HQ in Sacramento was putting massive pressure on them to open it up no matter what it took.

Sergeants (LE) Captains (in fire service) who are just supervisors, be willing to take any heat to keep your people and the public you are charged with protected and safe. It's better than living the rest of your life with the guilt if something goes horribly wrong. It was only by the grace of God and those pilots that we did not experience a disaster that day.

Sharpening the Axe

As time went on, I still didn't feel ready to jump right in and try to help or debrief somebody. I still had very pronounced PTSD symptoms of my own. I attended annual peer support training and any small tune-ups that were given.

To this day, I do not know why, but I would come home from each one extremely angry, except for two. One was a four-day presentation by a fellow named Kevin Gilmartin and the other was a one-day presentation by Robert Douglas.

I felt both of these presentations were what I had been looking for and were superior in every way to anything I had thus far tried. Both were former law enforcement from opposite sides of the country. Both were now psychologists brave enough to descend back into our world to help us make sense of emotional trauma and first-responder suicide and its effects on those left behind.

Gilmartin's presentation was his book: "Emotional Survival for Law Enforcement and Their Families." I do not have words to say how refreshing this was. Though this was not faith-based, I firmly believe it added years to my career and brought things into a much better focus. If you are a first responder, Gilmartin's presentation is a must, even if you are not struggling with trauma or PTSD, it puts things in a proper perspective.

Douglas' presentation was equally as enjoyable and effective except he delved down into the epidemic of first-responder suicide through his book or article: "The Pain and Suffering Created by First Responder Suicide." This started putting pieces together in my mind how and why we get to the edge and how quickly it can happen.

For the first time, I actually felt the CHP was serious about this epidemic. At the same time, this was helping me get it together and prepare myself to help others through Peer Support and any other way the Lord would bring them.

Soon after, I started getting phone calls in the middle of the night or randomly during the day from officers who had just experienced a crash where a child was killed or another traumatic incident that they could not shake. Each time, I was able to weave a small part of my own journey into empathy and understanding about what they had gone through, what they were going through, and what they were about to go through. I would try to let them know that it was okay to talk to a qualified professional. That there was no shame in seeking help and that seeking help can also make you stronger and give you an understanding and/or the ability to help others. Part of sharpening myself was also an understanding of simple statistics of law enforcement and firefighter suicide. I recall Gilmartin and Douglas giving out stats, but they were pertinent for that period of time.

In an article in the Statesman Journal of April 8. 2019, Capi Lynn revealed that PTSD and depression are five times higher in law enforcement and firefighters than in the civilian population. They are more likely to kill themselves than being killed in the line of duty by murder, traffic collisions, or fires.

She discussed a Ruderman study that in the U.S. in 2017, 140 police officers and 103 firefighters died by suicide, compared to 129 police officers and 93 firefighters who were killed in the line of duty. Another huge observation was that firefighter suicide is way underreported. The Behavioral Health Alliance estimated that only half of the firefighter suicides are reported. She goes on that the organization Blue Help reported that nationally, of the 460 law enforcement suicides from January 2016 to December 2018, California had 48 of them and that 37 percent were aged 40-49 and averaged seventeen years of service.

Her last point was one I already knew. You do not get a full honors funeral or your name in a granite monument if you commit suicide as a law enforcement officer or firefighter. Your final act is what you are most remembered for. You are broken down into cold, hard numbers. A nameless faceless statistic.

I mentioned earlier that during a 20-month period of time, CHP experienced 18 suicides in a 20-month period. There were a few that resigned and then suicided, so they were not included in that number.

"Mark"

I would like to put a face to one of my own officers who became a statistic and I refuse to allow his memory to be regarded as such.

I had been a sergeant for over a year and transferred into a new station. I knew some of the officers, sergeants, and the commander already. "Mark" was one I did not know. I noticed Mark was a bit edgy and almost unfriendly. Some of my guys told me he was having a real rough time at home. Father of two children, he had been living in his own garage for two years because his marriage was basically over, but he did not want to leave his kids.

The guys also told me he didn't like sergeants or brass, mostly because of the bad unfair experiences he'd had. I had worked the road with some of these guys and they knew I was not your ordinary sergeant.

The more I got to know Mark, the more I liked him. He was a darn good cop and could be counted on in any kind of circumstance. He transferred in from the central valley area known as Bakersfield. It was a super rough place, kind of like a miniature Los Angeles but with a country twist. He was also a top-flight auto mechanic and loved talking cars. I loved 60s muscle cars too and we had many good talks about them. I could tell the more he and I talked and interacted, the more he liked me. I could also tell he **didn't want** to like me. He saw that I protected my people, that I could let things slide, I could keep a confidence, and could be counted on for anything.

He knew much of my story and was aware that I knew some of his. He would say how he thought a lot about getting out of law enforcement and going back into "turning wrenches" as he put it. I saw a happy side to him on several occasions and it was encouraging to me.

However, there was a volatile side that flashed danger every time it surfaced. There was almost no controlling it. I could tell the stress and the career was catching up to him. He and I did get to the point that he knew he could tell me anything and that I would not take offense or get upset. I recall sitting in the sergeant's office wearing a heart monitor clipped to my gun belt. I was having more trouble with A-Fib and was a month or so away from surgery for it.

Mark came storming into the office and said in a raised voice, "What the hell is wrong with you?!"

I was puzzled and asked what he meant. He asked why I had not filed for medical retirement. I told him if I did, my family and I would lose our medical benefits. I also told him that I was forty-seven and needed to make it another three years for my pension at fifty.

Mark loudly pointed out that I could file legitimate claims on my back, neck, and heart, taking a year off on each one (standard work comp procedure in California).

"There is your three years!" He then said loudly, "Some of us are trapped here and have no way out and would give anything to be in your position!"

With that, he stormed out of my office. I understood exactly what he meant and why.

Many of us watched Mark struggle and tried to help, but you can only get so far with some people. Bad trouble at work translated into trouble off duty for him (as it almost always does with most people in this time of life). I transferred out of the office after about a year, but kept in loose contact. I had heard things were getting worse and the Department tried everything possible to help.

One day about a year later, I was at work and my commander came in and said that Mark had taken his own life. Things had snowballed and he felt he had no way out but to take his own life. I can't tell you how deeply Mark did care for others.

One of his best friends said, "Mark just didn't know how great he was."

Mark is not a statistic. He is a part of why I do this. I will not let his memory fade. His life means something to me and if I can pull someone back from the edge with his story, I will do it. I hope you found the peace you were seeking, brother.

Give God a Chance

How sad suicide must make God. Psalm 139:14 says, "We are fearfully and wonderfully made." In Jeremiah 29:11, God says, "I know the plans I have for you. Plans to prosper you and not harm you. Plans to give you hope and a good future."

Please give God a chance, especially when you feel like you are at the end of the road, and accept Him as your personal Lord and Savior and allow Him to do the rest.

I saw another statistic on a PSA on TV the other day that said each suicide has an adverse effect on an average of 150 people. I firmly believe that figure, but it's even worse for the immediate family. If a parent chooses suicide leaving young children behind, their chances of committing suicide exponentially increase.

Guide to Surviving in the Line of Duty

It was now that the training, the time in prayer asking God to use me, the Gilmartin and Douglas seminars, and my trove of personal experiences began to dovetail and take shape.

Read Psalm 40:1-2.

I believe God has sent medical doctors and licensed mental health professionals who are instrumental in helping us through the dark times.

If you have not already done so, I suggest reading or downloading:

Kevin Gilmartin's "Emotional Survival for Law Enforcement and Their Families."

Robert Douglas' "The Pain and Suffering Created by First Responder Suicide."

Perhaps, journal what you learn as they may help you help others as well.

I do not hear voices, but God let me know that He wanted me to help reach first responders (and anyone else who will listen) for Him, even if it was just a little bit and planting a seed. It would not be in an evangelistic sense, but instead, one or two at a time. He just wanted me to come alongside those who I can see are hurting or struggling, particularly in the first responder field, and help bear their load.

Is God calling you to come alongside someone you see struggling with tragedy or trauma in their life?

Will you respond to that call and ask God to give you the words to give them what they need?

> **"Come to me all you who are weary and heavy-laden, and I will give you rest."**
> **(Matthew 11:28)**

Chapter 5

CHANGE OF SCENERY AND PROMOTION

I BEGAN TO EXPERIENCE THE JOY OF THE Lord in my life in my career. I became the Public Information Officer at the Santa Barbara office, a position I had wanted since I was in the academy. I was double blessed to work for a commander that I went way back with and who cared deeply for his troops.

My wife had been pushing me for years to promote to sergeant. I resisted because, on the streets, it meant you crossed over to the dark side of the force and could no longer be trusted or included in anything. She would not let it go and as I got within six years of retirement, I could see the big boost promoting would give me on my pension check each month.

I finally took the sergeant's test two different times just to shut my wife up. The closer I got to retiring, the more I wanted that bump on my retirement check. I decided to get serious and transferred to the CHP Academy in West Sacramento and became an instructor in emergency medicine. Working out of a headquarters assignment is highly encouraged and is a big boost to your promotional chances.

I can't say how absolutely blessed I was to have landed where I did. The academy was huge. It was over 600 acres with many disciplines to teach in. I was permitted to live in a dorm that normally housed cadets, and that dorm was 30 feet from my office. I could not have asked for better office partners. The sergeant and the other two medics were as crazy and off the wall as I was. I not only learned volumes in emergency medicine, but I gained three very close friends for life. I was very leery of making close friends again, but these relationships came so naturally, I felt the Lord wanted me to start trusting people again.

We had approximately 500 cadets at any given time. We took care of their injuries and sicknesses and instructed them in their CPR, first aid, and did medical standby for their other functions. We were full advanced life support as well as administering the flight medic and flight nurse programs in our helicopters and SWAT teams. We also analyzed proposed bills from our lobby in Sacramento if they pertained to emergency medical service in any way.

Change of Scenery and Promotion

It was an amazing and welcome change of pace. I would recommend it to anybody who may be suffering burnout in the first responder field. My office partner and I were given 100 percent support from our sergeant and command staff for studying for the upcoming sergeant's exam. I recall not going home for a couple of months, just taking the time to study.

During this time, I was still experiencing some heavy PTSD symptoms, nightmares, intrusive thoughts, flashbacks, and anger. I would go home on Friday afternoons, drive the 360+ miles, and come back on Sunday evenings.

While I was gone, I asked my daughters thirteen and five to keep the dog and cat food and water full. Many times, I would come home, and it was very low or empty. I became increasingly outraged each time. I figured out, years later, that small things tend to magnify with PTSD. Unfortunately, I would let it all out at my family in the form of yelling, berating, and not letting anything go. I would also see that there had been no cleaning done. I would start in on the cleaning as well as the yard work. It made for terrible weekends.

I recall coming home one Friday night, walking through the door to see my daughters watching TV and on the computer. They both looked at me, but said nothing and just went back to what they were doing. I needed help realizing that these were precious times in life with my girls. It was time I was not going to ever get back and it did years of damage. My wife would try to intervene or calm things, but I would jump all over her. I hated coming home and they hated having me home. I don't blame them.

> **If this is happening to you, please stop. You are doing irreparable harm and driving those you need the most away from you.**

More Loss

On the morning of August 29, 2009, I was home on days off from the academy when my phone rang. It was a friend of mine who worked out of the San Diego CHP Office. He worked with a very close friend and academy classmate of mine named Mark Saylor. He was very shaken up and he told me Mark, his wife, thirteen-year-old daughter, and his brother-in-law were killed in a tragic traffic accident the previous night.

I was so shocked that I didn't even understand what he was telling me. He broke down and told me they had been driving a loaner Lexus from the dealership where their car was being serviced. They were on a highway that ended in a "T" intersection with another highway. Suddenly, the car accelerated on its own to over 100 mph and crashed, bursting into flames when

Change of Scenery and Promotion

it ran off the road and into a small ravine at the end of the highway.

This crash made world news and set the stage for the lawsuits against Toyota/Lexus for several more collisions with the same cause.

I had the honor of being one of Mark's pallbearers at the funeral. I was flooded with emotion, memories of Mark, sadness for him and his wife's families, and intrusive thoughts from the deaths of Rick and Britt eleven years earlier. I had thoughts about how rocky my own home life was that just created a tsunami of undealt with stuff. I didn't have time for it and stuffed it the best I could, but stress cracks were already starting to appear.

Mark and I had reported to the CHP Academy on May 15, 1989. We could not have been more different. He was from the big city of St. Louis, Missouri, and I was from a very small town on the central coast of California, San Luis Obispo. Both our fathers were policemen in our hometowns, and we were both addicted to old television shows, but that is where the similarities ended. We were in separate companies in the academy, but were both sent to the same station in Los Angeles, where we became very close.

As soon as we were able, we partnered up on the graveyard shift for six months. We were the same age. I went to college, and he went into the Air Force. He was the funniest person I ever met. At the end of each shift, my face and stomach hurt from laughing so hard.

He introduced me to African American humor, which I found that I loved. He even practiced it while we were on the job. I remember he loved James Brown and when it was my turn to balance somebody out on the sidewalk for possible DUI, he would stand about fifteen feet behind the person and take out his baton, use it as a microphone, gyrating his hips, and sing and dance just like James Brown. He would also flare his knees in and out when he sang, "Papa's Got A Brand New Bag."

We found we both loved making fun of each other, arrestees, and people we worked with behind their backs. We especially enjoyed discussing how they resembled famous figures. We worked with a guy who bore a remarkable resemblance to Vanilla Ice. We would sneak up behind him and his partner and do a drive-by when they were out on stops and Mark would tap the tune of one of Vanilla Ice's songs on the loudspeaker microphone as we slowly cruised by. When one of us would say, "Hey, he looks like…" the other already knew.

We played on the same office softball team. He was a very gifted player and played on the CHP police Olympic championship team that went to Japan. We also shared a lot of close personal stuff, as you would imagine. We laughed together and got in trouble together. We even stopped Easy-E, twice, together. Mark had to point out who he was both times because I was the approaching officer.

After two years of working together, I transferred out to Santa Maria. He stayed a few more years then transferred to San Diego. As you would figure, we lost touch. I called him about eight months before he was killed and visited a while, but we never found the time to get together.

I am sure some of you are thinking of that car partner or partner on the rig that you were once very close with but have let that friendship lapse. Put this book down right now and give them a shout. Make some plans, just don't let those good friendships go.

Promotion, a Miracle, and a Lobotomy that Didn't Take

I know what you road dogs and veteran rig hounds are thinking. How could you go over to the dark side of supervision and leave your people languishing on the streets? I have to say it was a combination of many forces.

1. To get my wife off my back.
2. For the pay increase and the increase on the retirement check.
3. I worked, literally, for the worst the department had to offer, and I felt if I just did things opposite what they did, I would be a success.
4. In the second half of my career, I was blessed to work for and with some wonderful people who

cared and showed me it was okay to care about those who would work for me.

I chose to make good use of my time at the academy, pouring hundreds of hours into studying. Lots of people laughed at my unorthodox studying style, but I came out #25 on a list of hundreds with over 1,200 taking the test. I prayed very hard for God's will and that He would use me for Him in a great and mighty way to help others and be a good witness for Him. I would not have done it, scored so high, and done so well without God's help, and the support of my office partners, sergeant, management, and command staff.

I was able to be the first to officially promote off my list. Usually, on the CHP, you have to leave and go back to the big city for every promotion. Again, I was blessed and got a very small office/station in Monterey County in King City.

God blessed me as I was able to live with my grandfather 70 miles south of King City, but I had to return to Santa Barbara Area for some "acting sergeant" practice first.

Santa Barbara was the same place I had left. I encountered a great staff from top to bottom. I gained about five months of good office supervision experience, until my last day before reporting to King City. I was out driving my old beat on the 101 freeway as it runs along the Pacific Ocean. I came upon a disabled vehicle with an older man and woman on the right shoulder. Through dispatch, I called AAA and was just saying goodbye after telling them the tow would be there in 20 minutes. I looked back at approaching traffic and I could not believe what I saw.

There was a full-size 18-wheel big rig heading off the roadway directly at us. The big rig tractor was missing its right front tire and rim. What was worse, there was fire over 15 feet high pouring out of where the wheel and rim had once been. I had a full view of the driver. His eyes were shut, and his head was slightly turned to the left with his teeth showing as he braced for impact. His hands were on the steering wheel cranked over to the left, not moving, and it looked as though he was fearing the worst.

I was just frozen and couldn't move. I kept watching, but instead of impact, I watched that entire rig move at the last possible second as if it were gently nudged back out into the slow lane of traffic, passed us, and then moved just as smoothly back onto the right shoulder. As it passed, I had just enough time to turn away as I felt the intense heat all over my body and through my Kevlar vest, just like the wildfire years before.

As it came to rest, both diesel tanks ruptured and began leaking fuel onto the right shoulder, heading straight for the drain that drained directly out to the ocean. In California law enforcement, one way to buy yourself months of paperwork is to let a drop of any spilled substance reach any waterway.

Having that in mind, I grabbed a shovel and made an earthen dam that stopped the diesel literally 6-8 inches from the storm drain. As I was trying to make sense of what I had just seen happen, I was about to find out the miracle was not over.

I was told I had no help coming, so I went out in the slow lane, closing it down with cones. What I did not know was that the 200+ pound big-rig rim and tire were now on fire just up the hill in the brush behind us.

I heard a very loud explosion come from behind me. With traffic still going by in the fast lane, I thought there was another crash. I turned quickly to see the rim and tire, now fully engulfed, fly about 75 feet into the air and land about 3-5 feet from me in between both lanes. Using my patrol unit's fire extinguisher, I was able to put the tire fire out. I had to stop for a moment and take it all in.

I realized the Lord had performed two miracles:

1. He spared me, yet again, (and those people in the car).
2. Nobody was hit by the flying, burning big-rig tire and rim which would have been certain death.

The Lord kept me going in the moment, but as soon as it was all over, I pondered and pondered. I asked the Lord, "Why was I spared again? Why do I deserve such protection?" The only thing that came to me was the part of Psalm 91 where it says, "He will give His angels charge over you, to guard you in all your ways." I was humbled and felt very undeserving, knowing God keeps His promises.

> **God protected me because He promised He would in His Word, thousands of years ago. He never changes. He said that He is the same yesterday, today, and forever and if He never changes, neither does His Word.**

I felt like He was just pointing out that He was just keeping His word, but at the same time, I knew this wasn't all He was doing. There was an unshakeable feeling that there was far more. A reinforcement, I guess, that the Lord wanted me to use what He had done for me to further His saving grace. It was a reminder that He was sending me into a vast mission field that was in desperate need of laborers who not only cared, but who had lived through and been saved from what they were and would be going through.

I reported to King City CHP in September of 2010. It was a more junior and much smaller station/office than Santa Barbara. Again, I was blessed with an office of really great people. The vast majority of the officers were squared-away and top-notch who took care of their own. Some of the middle seniority officers were not afraid to speak their minds and I secretly liked and respected that. I was never hung up on my sergeant stripes and I communicated that to the officers in every station I worked from then on.

I wanted them to know I wanted them to talk to me as they would their own beat partners. Call me if you have a problem. The best solutions to problems out there always came from the field folks. I always wanted to know how my folks were doing and if there was ever anything I could do to make it better.

I guess what I am trying to say is that my mind never got out of the "officer" gear. My experiences over the years played a major part in that. I was told from the get-go that I could no longer be friends with or as close to my officers even if I had chewed the same dirt with them out on the road. I watched as those I worked with conformed to this dogma. It cost them respect and most importantly, the trust of the officers.

I knew in my heart of hearts I could still care and look out for my folks as much or more than I ever had, and still be a great sergeant, but by whose standards? I knew my philosophy would not comport with what management was shoveling and it didn't. In all the stations/offices where I was a sergeant, I got the distinct feeling of being considered the least effective by supervision and command's measure. Yes, it bothered me a few times, but it was a price I was willing to pay. I took things in the back for my people and sometimes never told them. I knew in whose hearts and minds my legacy mattered most.

The CHP, like most other public safety departments, sent newly promoted supervisors to a three-week Front-line Supervisors' Academy, commonly known as the "Lobotomy." Over the years, I watched many a good officer go into this Bermuda Triangle, and come out the other side as a totally different person, and not for the better.

My experience was good. There was a lot of good, useful information, but we were also handed the line, "These people are not your friends," meaning those we would be supervising. I begged to differ and told the captain so in front of the class, letting him know some of the people I would be supervising had been through the same deep water I had and our bonds were stronger than the stripes I was wearing.

> **The biggest advice I would give any newly promoted first responder supervisor is to put those who work for you first and do whatever they need or want immediately.**

The King City station/office was a great place for me to break in as a new sergeant. It was slow as far as the day-to-day events went, but strangely, it was a very active place.

The Norteno and Sureno boundary line for the whole state went right through the middle of town on Broadway Ave. Consequently, there were a very high number of murders in the small city that went unsolved. I heard one happen from my desk one day.

Many of you are wondering what I just said. The terms Norteno and Sureno pertain to a large number of Hispanic gangs in California. Norteno means Northerners and surenos mean Southerners. Try to imagine it as a fast-food franchise. If you are operating a Hispanic gang north of Broadway in King City, you were a Norteno. You were allied with all other Hispanic gangs in the northern part of the state and paid your proceeds from your drug dealing, theft, and other illicit behavior to the main people in charge which would be the Mexican Mafia.

Conversely, If you lived and operated a Hispanic gang south of Broadway in King City, you owed the proceeds from drugs and other illicit behavior to those who controlled the southern portion of the state which was MS 13. The boundary itself could be fluid, but at the time, it was Broadway Ave.

For such a small town, gang activity was very high. I listened and learned a lot from my officers about tactics and SWAT stacks! Yes, I was floored to learn we were regularly going into houses with the small PDs and Monterey County Sheriff's Dept. With the high gang activity and violence, the police and sheriff were spread way too thin. Part of our mission was to assist allied agencies and my officers were the first to step up. My heart used to swell when I heard my folks on the air, heading in to back up their brothers and sisters. I was very proud of them and let them know about it every chance I got.

I began to seriously worry when because of massive budget shortfalls, the sheriff's department had to virtually pull out of southern Monterey County, which meant our King City substation. The choice that confronted the sheriff's department was faced with was to pull out of south county or close the jail. This left the small police departments on their own and the tiny outlying communities relying on us with a very extended response time of an hour or more for the sheriff.

At 2 A.M., the morning after Thanksgiving of 2010, I got a phone call from my only graveyard unit. They had a double gang-related homicide with a scene that stretched several miles and spilled onto the freeway. They were being told it was theirs to handle. It was all straightened out in the end, but times were very lean.

In King City, three days before I retired, a Norteno gang member, on foot, took several shots at a passing car in a heavily populated neighborhood, right in front of a King City Police Department Commander on her way home from work. The shooter ran inside a house that was not his, causing the elderly lady owner to come running outside.

The call came to us for assistance. I had three beat units and three overtime units. I was the first to arrive (sound familiar?). The KCPD commander stuck around long enough to tell me what had happened and then disappeared, leaving a single KCPD officer who had just gotten off FTO a few days before, and us.

I set up a perimeter and managed to get one other allied agency officer to respond, but that was it. I requested the Sheriff's SWAT team. They declined to come out, leaving just us. I phoned my commander and explained what was happening and that the elderly lady was terrified to go back into her own house and no help was coming. Our commander totally got it. It was an awesome feeling knowing we had the full support of our commander. Even though we didn't even have a dog in this fight, we were going to help this elderly woman get safely back into her home. After hours of using the bull horn and hovering the helicopter with the infrared FLIR trying to contact the shooter to no avail, we decided to go in there and take on whoever it was.

Suddenly, I began to get a weird feeling of apprehension. Here I am three days from retirement, and I am stacking up to go inside this house after an armed gang banger who has just taken shots at people. Then somebody said the obvious.

"Hey, Sarge, this is where you usually buy it in all the movies, just before retirement."

As we were stacking up, I said a quick prayer, called my wife, and left a message. The moment I uttered that prayer, I was flooded with peace. At first, I thought, "God, is this what one feels just before they buy it?" The feeling was very different after my prayer, "I have protected you all your life, especially since you pinned on that badge. Why would I fail you now? I have a plan for your life. You are going to reach people for Me."

Can God give you feelings that complex without words? He can. He did. He is always there with you.

Fire guys, when you are the first in and last out of that burning house, God is there with you. The greater the danger, the stronger His presence. I remember times of dire need. I felt His presence so overwhelmingly, I had to keep myself from looking to my right because I felt the presence of God so close. I knew there was a good chance I would be allowed to see my guardian angel or St. Michael, the Archangel of God right there next to me.

I can't describe it other than an overwhelmingly powerful feeling that will help you stick in the fight when people are trying to assault you and defund you. It will help you overcome anything that comes your way. Then, when the action is all gone and the enemy is coming at you about everything you have experienced, God is still there to carry you through any fire, chase away the PTSD, and give you back to your families, whole.

Guide to Surviving in the Line of Duty

I can't describe God's presence other than an overwhelmingly powerful feeling that will help you stick in the fight when people are trying to assault you and defund you. It will help you overcome anything that comes your way. Then, when the action is all gone and the enemy is coming at you about everything you have experienced, God is still there to carry you through any fire, chase away the PTSD, and give you back to your families, whole.

Read Psalm 91.

> **God protected me because He promised He would in His Word, thousands of years ago. He never changes. He said that He is the same yesterday, today, and forever and if He never changes, neither does His Word.**

As you think back over the unexplainable times you have felt protected when you were in the line of fire, do you see where it was God keeping His promise?

Can you now see it was God's presence protecting and keeping you?

> **Can God give you feelings that complex without words? He can. He did. He is always there with you.**

Chapter 6

TRANSFER BACK TO SANTA MARIA AND LOOKING EVIL IN THE EYE

I KNOW WHAT YOU'RE THINKING, "AM I NUTS?" Maybe so, but it is true that the Lord works in strange ways. To be closer to my family, I transferred back to Santa Maria, but this time as a sergeant. A few old friends were still there I had worked with and found it to be a solid veteran squad with topflight folks and a commander I had enjoyed working the road with back in the day. Once again, I considered myself blessed.

I liked being back in Santa Maria but felt it a bit odd supervising old friends. I was indeed blessed because these guys really didn't need supervising. My atrial fibrillation was getting worse, and I found myself wearing a heart monitor that I had to clip to my gun belt. The monitor was hooked up to 24/7 live monitoring from out of state. I would get calls in the middle of the night, at church, or at the movies asking if I was feeling what was happening.

I was trying to hold my own, knowing I only had three years left until I could retire and if this ablation could fix things, that would be great. I thought the ablation could fix the heart, but it could not fix the mind.

Mother's Day morning 2012, I had been working overtime about fifty miles out of town on Old Highway 166. I had been on for 14-15 hours and was on my way back to the station when a fatality accident, auto versus pedestrian came out just two miles from me. Both of my graveyard units were busy and, you guessed it, I was first on the scene. The responsible vehicle had fled the scene but left the headless male's body in the middle of the road.

The man was homeless, and I felt bad that he probably would not be missed. I was wrong. He had a family and a mother who cared about him but had not heard from him in years. I ended up working twenty-seven hours that day. Even that tired, sleep was hard to come by. I kept thinking of the man's mother being given the news of her son's death and that every Mother's Day from now on would no longer be a celebration, but a reminder. How many Mother's Days had she already spent worrying?

I did my best to try keeping my head above water, but kept noticing cracks beginning to form. I was "weepy," crying at a drop of a hat, and equally irritable, especially at home. I kept going to church each Sunday and did my best to have my devotional time with the Lord, but I had no fellowship with any other believers or anybody else, for that matter. I had been isolating myself for years. My stress-related illnesses were at their peak. I just needed to make it another three years.

When at work, I was the happiest when I was out on the road, alone, or in the sergeant's office alone. One particular Sunday afternoon, I had been in the sergeant's office for over six hours doing a mountain of paperwork when I decided to go out, drive around, and relax. A broadcast came out over the radio that was an urgent Code 3 backup for the sheriff's department, approximately twenty miles away.

Our dispatch was connected to a hardcore gangbanger who was on methamphetamine and alcohol. He was driving a car with his girlfriend and two-year-old child. The girlfriend got on the phone and said he had a large knife and was trying to stab her and the child by lunging at them with the knife. He could be heard saying he was going to do something bad and then go out by suicide by cop. He said all of his friends had been killed by the police.

The girl would give locations where they were which was by a small community. As usual, we had the whole world coming, but nobody was close.

John Wayne once said, "The definition of brave was being scared to death but saddling up and riding in anyway." I felt nauseous. After working the streets for so long, there is a feeling you get in your gut that this is not going to end well. I had an actual adrenaline dump because I felt total anxiety in my arms and legs, but my body took over and I sped over 120 mph toward the last location. I could tell by the radio traffic that I was, by far, the closest as I approached the small community they were near.

My beat unit was in the area and I knew the suspect was in one of two locations. Both needed to be checked. Just from the description, I knew he had to be north of town by a few miles, but the chance remained he may be south. My beat unit had very young children and I purposely had him check south of town. I have never said this to anyone until now, but I did not want to see another brother dead on my shift.

If he didn't find anything, he would only be a few minutes behind me. I was praying hard, really hard. My stomach was still nauseous, but my heart was going in and out of A-Fib. He was still yelling on the phone that he was going to do something bad. I passed the third mile north of town and rounded a curve in the two-lane road. I saw him stopped and outside the car.

I was once again, first on scene and alone. The male suspect was outside the vehicle looking and yelling at his girlfriend who was standing outside with her back up against the open driver's door, screaming. I saw the suspect's shirt had blood on it, but it was what I did not see that scared me even more. I did not see the two-year-old child. My mind was racing. I knew the suspect said he was going to do something bad and go out by suicide by cop. I thought the blood belonged to the child and that he was going to attack his girlfriend or me.

As soon as he saw me, he turned fully to face me and began advancing toward me at a quick pace. I had to put it out that I had found them, where we were, ascertain what was in his hand, bail out of the patrol car, and decide how to counter him, protect myself, his girlfriend, and the child.

I did not want to give him his wish to go suicide by cop. He kept screaming, "You killed my friends," over and over. Only later did I find out that he was the sole survivor of several hard-core gangster friends who had taken on the different police departments and sheriff's department. All had gone the same route he was choosing. There had been something like six fatal law enforcement shootings in two weeks in our small geographical area.

What I had heard about shooting incidents was true. Everything slowed way down, and I couldn't hear anything around me except the suspect yelling that I had killed his friends. I was standing behind my driver's door just as he came to the front of my car. I could see the object in his left hand was a large folding knife. It was open and I could see blood on it. I was yelling at him to get back and drop the knife, but he kept coming. He was now within 8-12 feet of me. I knew I was totally justified in using my service weapon, but I did not want to kill him. I decided to try to shoot the hand that was raised with the knife in it.

As I began to squeeze the trigger, things really slowed down. The hammer seemed like it came back in slow motion. I shot twice and saw the rounds hit his left hand and do their damage. The suspect just growled at me and kept advancing toward me with the knife still raised in his injured hand. In my mind, I could hear our gruff rangemaster say "Move!" I gave ground and ran back to the left rear corner of my patrol car. He charged forward and slammed my driver's door closed and raised his knife again, coming directly at me. I shot three more times just to wound and stop him. He stood there growling and swaying for what seemed like a very long time and 8-10 feet from me and he finally went down, the knife still in his hands. As he hit the ground, the knife fell out of his hand and landed just about between my feet.

I had no idea, but just as the first shot was going off, backup had arrived, but things were happening so fast that it was over before they could get into action. My heart was beating outside my chest, but I could feel it going in and out of atrial fib. Since I was the shift supervisor, I had to make my own notification calls to the higher-ups.

I was feeling very overwhelmed with life as it was and now this? I knew what was ahead for the rest of the evening. I was transported to a location across town where I had to wait in a room for 3-4 hours for the investigating agency (sheriff) to finish up at the scene and then come to interrogate me. Before that, I had to have numerous pictures taken of me and my gear for the investigation. Finally, the sheriff investigators were there for my interrogation, but I would have to sit for the district attorney's interrogation and my own department's interrogation.

By now my heart was slipping more and more into A-Fib. I finally got to call my wife and let her know and asked her to bring my heart medication so I could take another dose. By now the meds were no longer working very well. I was not allowed to see my wife until I got home in the early morning hours the next day.

I was treated very well by all three agencies with the D.A. sitting in on the sheriff's interview. My representative was an old hat at this and was one of my old sergeants. I felt good that I was within the law for what I had done. However, I felt sick to my stomach that I had to do it, even though I gave the guy every opportunity to stop. I knew he was about to use his knife on me to make me kill him. I was praying hard for him to be okay.

I walked out of there around 2 or 3 in the morning and was greeted by a sergeant and fellow peer support team member. He was really glad to see me and put it all into perspective when he said, "Now, I was the only guy he knew who had checked every box in the trauma department, some multiple times." He also told me the suspect was still alive.

I remember replying, "Good! I was praying for him."

He ended up pulling through, but with extreme permanent complications. He received seven years in prison but was out in about three-and-a-half. He has been back since, in and out of trouble. I have never stopped praying for him that the Lord would get ahold of his life and use him in a great and mighty way to pull kids like him, (he was eighteen), off the street, out of the gangs, and turn them to Christ.

I got home and was pleasantly surprised when my wife put her arms around me and told me she loved me. That kind of affection between us had been missing for a very long time and it felt good for a moment.

Jaws were on the ground when I was right back to work. I felt that time off after a shooting was for this newer more "tender" generation. I remember saying that back in my day, we didn't need time off.

In the coming days, I tried faking that I was okay. The truth was I felt like a miserable wreck and weepy. I was having all sorts of nightmares. Nightmares that I was in desperate shooting situations and that I had my duty weapon, but the trigger was frozen and too hard to pull. Everything was in super slow motion, but the assailants were in real-time. I would only wake up just about the time I would die or get shot. I would also have dreams that I was off duty, but I would interrupt an armed robbery or an attempted murder. Every time, I would sneak up on the suspect and grab him by the neck or head. I would then put my gun up to their ear and just begin shooting and not stop until I felt their warm brains oozing down my arm.

I was trying to get passed that incident, but I was suffering every kind of physical and emotional PTSD side effect you can name. I was being offered time off, but each time I would reply, no. Truth was that I needed it more than I knew.

Only fifteen days later, I was on my afternoon shift and dispatch put out a call for Code 3 assistance for the sheriff and the PD on an armed robbery suspect. They were in a slow-speed pursuit going up the main drag of town in a heavily populated area. It was so slow, some people were riding up and keeping up on bicycles on the sidewalk to look to their left, right, or side-ways to see who it was.

I was at my desk and heard it come out over the air. It sounded as though there was a sheriff and a PD unit officially in the pursuit. One of our veteran officers was not in it, but was hanging back, attempting to keep "looky-loos" away. We were advised the subject was armed with at least one gun, maybe more.

The roadway pursuit ended at a river levy and a dead end. The suspect turned his vehicle around as if to head in the opposite direction, but was sandwiched in by two or three PD and sheriff units. There was still a possibility he could squeeze through an opening, but my unit who had been keeping the curious at bay, filled it.

The activity was so close to the freeway that by this time, I and three more of my units were formed up on the freeway in case the suspect headed that direction. Once we were certain the pursuit was no longer moving, we responded to the scene with the rest of my units blocking off the surface street in case the suspect came back that way. I drove up to the standoff to see only three officers with guns drawn, holding back the suspect, who was still in his vehicle, facing them. There was an immediate need for one more officer and I took up the position, waiting for more PD or sheriff to arrive.

As I stood there with my own gun drawn, the sheriff was giving the suspect commands to throw out his gun and exit his vehicle. I had a million things running through my mind. I needed to immediately advise my commander, get myself and my other officer out of the standoff, and be replaced by PD or sheriff. I also noticed I was in full-sustained atrial fibrillation and could hardly stand. I prayed for strength. It also dawned on me that I was about to get into yet another shooting.

Transfer Back to Santa Maria and Looking Evil in the Eye

By now, an allied agency officer arrived and replaced me on the line. I holstered and was relieved I would not be shooting again.

More help was en route, but I couldn't safely pull my officer off the line, so I called my commander and was in the process of advising him of all the circumstances when I noticed most of the neighborhood had emptied out of their homes and were attempting to watch. This was very dangerous, and I was yelling for them to get back inside and trying to communicate with my commander at the same time while in full A-fib. The suspect was surging his vehicle at us like he was going to try breaking through the line of patrol cars.

At this time, the suspect had thrown a handgun out of his vehicle and had exited. He had been shouting profanity at the officers and still was as he stood outside. He bent down and picked his gun back up and pointed it under his chin. Now the shouting increased. I was still desperately trying to get the citizens back into their homes and talk to my commander.

Suddenly, the suspect pointed the gun at the line of officers and that was it. There was a hail of gunfire. Again, things seemed to slow down. It was as if the suspect was just standing there. I saw flesh flying off him from the bullet impacts as he crumpled straight down.

I wanted to throw up again. I was experiencing the same feelings I had fifteen days earlier except this time my heart was making my whole body feel as if it were on a non-stop roller coaster going straight down. I almost fainted from the dizziness, but knew if I did, I would be medically retired and my family and I would lose all of our medical insurance. (Great way to treat first responders who become medically unable to work isn't it? The public never hears this.)

I now had to try to act okay. The sergeant from the neighboring CHP area was at the scene in its final moments. He was the one who had done a good job sitting with me just fifteen days before during my own shooting interrogation.

However, this time he walked up with one of his officers and said, "You're done, Dan, you're done!" and he left.

By now it was only the Lord keeping me going. My commander arrived along with our sector chief. Thankfully, both these guys got it and their concern was just about us. I had so much to say, but they were too busy and I probably could not have gotten it all out anyway. I was lucky that I was just inches outside the "shooting scene" and was one of the first interviewed by the same investigators from two weeks earlier and was allowed to go home.

I did not get the same greeting I had two weeks earlier from my wife. It was more like, "Don't turn the lights on when you come to bed."

I returned to work, just trying to keep my nose above water, but was no longer even running on fumes. I was completely out of gas. My medication for my A-fib only partially controlled it and I would have to fight my way through each day.

I was able to get through the next few months. My commander was a guy I had worked the road with and known for just under twenty years. He was constantly checking on me, which made me feel good, but at the same time, I could tell he knew I was in a tailspin. By now, my cardiologist had me scheduled for ablation at Stanford, but the date was two months away. I was scheduled to go to our academy for Advanced Officer Safety Training. It was a weeklong, intense martial arts tactics course. I was supposed to set the example for our guys to come and take the course. I was still on my heart meds, wearing a heart monitor, and taking blood thinners because I was going into A-fib so much.

The course was extremely hands-on, with lots of sparring, grappling, striking, firearms drills, and anything else you can think of. The instructors were outstanding, and I actually enjoyed it, up until the last day when we used all our skills in practical scenarios. (If you haven't guessed by now, yes, something bad happens. It's okay to laugh. Really.)

Before we launched into our scenarios, we were briefed that the actors would go full hands-on and that they loved to fight. My turn rolled around and a guy came out of a building in a full padded suit which meant one thing: there was going to be a fight. Sure enough, in a moment we were going at it. I remember I was about to kick with my right foot when I felt something deep inside my right calf area, slowly tear, and suddenly snap.

The pain was intense, and I went down just as the scenario came to an end. I looked down and my calf was as big as my thigh. They called for our EMS, who was my old office partner and close friend. His face sank when he got to me because he knew what a train wreck I already was.

He didn't waste any time and loaded me up in the EMS vehicle and took me directly into the UC Davis Emergency room. He had no place to park and I walked into the ER on my own power. The young intern who greeted me took one look at my leg and started to panic and said, "I gotta go get my boss!" He turned around and ran.

Within five minutes, I had seven doctors around my bed. They were shooting me with all kinds of pain meds, but they didn't work. Their faces changed when I told them I was on blood thinners and a cardiac patient. They thought I was looped or out of it and held a consultation at the foot of my bed.

I heard one say, "We gotta get this guy into surgery stat."

Another one said, "We've never heard of the blood thinner he's on and the pharmacy says if we cut into him, he could just keep bleeding."

I turned and looked at my old office partner who was now sitting next to my bed and both our mouths flew open. The next thing I knew I was being wheeled into surgery. Somebody was writing something on my leg and I sat up to see what it was. Suddenly, I felt a hand go over my forehead and plop my head back down and that was it.

I came to in recovery and was wheeled out to the cardiac floor where I got to hear people code at 5:30 each morning. The head surgeon came in and said I had suffered a muscle tear that went into compartment syndrome. Because of the blood thinners, I started bleeding internally and the blood cut off my circulation to the lower part of my leg. He said I came within about ten minutes of having my leg amputated from below the knee down and that I was very lucky. I saw two tubes coming out of my right calf with gunk flowing out. The surgeon said I would have to stay in the hospital for a week and have one more surgery.

I received the best care from the most wonderful people, but I had nothing but time to sit, think, and worry. I actually felt mentally better because I was told this would keep me off work for six months or so. I began to do the math. It would still leave me short of turning fifty years old and being able to retire. I knew I would have to go back at some point.

I was able to physically escape being at work, but mentally was another issue. The dreams kept coming and extreme intrusive thoughts of violence from the recent past. Loud noises would cause me to jump. It was a long six days and a second surgery. Suddenly, I found myself possibly marooned almost 400 miles from home with no way home. I asked the CHP for a ride home since I was injured on the job, but was told no. It wasn't until I found out a fire captain from my church in Santa Barbara County was up in Sacramento for training. He was happy to give me a ride home.

Guide to Surviving in the Line of Duty

> "God moves in a mysterious way, His wonders to perform." — William Cowper[3]

Read Isaiah 55:8-9.

I believe God has sent medical doctors and licensed mental health professionals who are instrumental in helping us through the dark times. Instead of trying to fake or just push through as I did, you need to allow those who God sends your way to help you and potentially save your life.

The doctor told me I came within about ten minutes of having my leg amputated from below the knee down and that I was very lucky.

Please learn from my mistakes.

---

[3] God Moves in a Mysterious Way - Wikipedia

Chapter 7

BACK TO THE RUBBER GUN SQUAD

I TRANSFERRED BACK TO THE BUELLTON Area. It had been several years, but again, I was very blessed. The commander was an academy classmate of mine and a first-rate guy. The squad was extremely senior and was so good that they would have any scene already stabilized before I would ever get there.

One particular day, I had only two officers for an area of 800-1200 square miles. A big rig truck crashed, and an Haz-Mat spill ensued. Sergeants are responsible for heading up, working, and reporting in writing for the whole thing. When the call came out, I was in the office. I put my belt on, grabbed my gear, and I drove up to the scene. It only took me 10-15 minutes, but I found my guys had already coned off the lanes and gathered all the necessary paperwork and statements.

One of them just handed everything to me and started laughing because he knew it was a solid two days' worth of paperwork, and he drove off to have coffee. We need to treasure people like this and keep them happy. They are a big factor in making you, as a supervisor, shine.

From day one, my commander would regularly check in with me. Since we went so far back, he could see I was struggling just with day-to-day tasks. The intrusive thoughts were now also intrusive scenes. My cracks were getting bigger. I would find myself crying even more at small things or for no reason at all.

At home, things were no better. Conflict with my wife was more the norm than the exception. We were living in a guest house on a lavender farm. We had traded two years of rent in exchange for remodeling the guest house. Just as we finished, the owner decided to back out and say it was only worth half of our agreed-upon price.

This seemed to be a tipping point. I could barely function. For years, I had referred our folks going through the effects of extreme trauma to a place in the mountains of northern California called West Coast Post Trauma Retreat. It was a six-day in-patient program for first responders who are at the end of the line. The doctors and clinicians are all former cops and firefighters who are on a second career. You are surrounded by 10-20 peers. These are also first responders who have gone through trauma and the program.

They only take 6-7 patients at a time and each patient is assigned two peers. It is the most intense six days you will ever spend.

I noticed nothing mattered anymore. I had quit doing anything like a hobby or of interest years earlier. (They call this "The used tos." I used to do this or I used to do that). What was very alarming was that I had completely stopped thinking about or noticing my family, and I lived with them! I no longer cared about anything or anyone and I was not surprised when I finally realized I didn't want to live anymore.

It was at this particular point that I had an overwhelming urge to start looking down the barrel of my service weapon. I noticed how the jacketed hollow point gleamed against the shiny rifled barrel. I had no urge to touch or pull the trigger, but I just kept doing it, mostly at work. This did not last long until I noticed I seemed to quickly accelerate downhill into a darkness where I found I could not even talk to anybody. I really wanted to feel better. I really wanted to talk to somebody, but I could not think of who. I did not want to talk to anyone I knew because I did not want them to know how messed up I was and I was pretty sure nobody else would really understand where I was and how I felt. I was also in constant ceaseless pain in my low back from the rigors of the job that was now taking its toll.

A big flashing red light came when I reasoned that it was just too much work to try to find anyone and that this would all pass like it always had. What I didn't realize was that I was completely at peace with that decision. My thoughts and entire outlook became darker, and my dreams were very dark, mostly centering around death and violence.

I hit a point where this seemed to accelerate and I didn't care. Everything seemed like a blur or surreal until a still, small voice deep inside told me I was screwed up and at an extremely dangerous point in my life, mentally.

It took all I had to tell my commander where I was and to make the necessary phone calls to get in line for West Coast. My commander and our association could not have been better in contacting the right people to get me into the program.

I remember the 5-6 hour drive up to the house where WCPTR was held. I almost turned around several times before arriving. When I arrived I sat in my truck and did not even take the keys out because I was still thinking about leaving. I think they had one of the clinicians patrolling the parking area for just that reason because I looked up and there he was.

He wasted no time in telling me to take the keys out and follow him, in a lighthearted way. It was an absolutely beautiful setting in the hills of Napa. Everyone was friendly as they trickled in. I could tell some were there as peers because they seemed a bit wacko. (When you're messed up, it's easier to spot someone else who is also.) I remember not liking the friendliness and I knew that was wrong because it wasn't like me.

We assembled and got into the introductions. I looked around the room wondering who was the most messed up. I knew there was nobody in that room who could relate to my situation, especially being responsible for the deaths of two of my partners. I was actually very surprised to find one of the peers who had killed a fellow officer from his own department in an undercover raid gone bad. This was comforting to me, but after the first or second day, I do not recall seeing him again. Still, I knew I was in the right place and that this is where God wanted me because He was to use it as part of my testimony.

Immediately after the introductions, the lead doctor looked right at me and said, "Never, in the history of this place have we had so many very high-ranking people from a department try for so long to get someone in here as we have had with you, Dan."

My six-day stay was the most intense of my life. I wondered if we were going to be in bathrobes and play badminton like you see mental patients portrayed in the movies.

It was a combination of education about PTSD, its effects, strategies, treatment, and how to become whole again. Part of this was each of us dealing with all of our demons in front of each other, head-on. This was done with the doctors and therapists only.

One of the most beneficial therapies was the use of EMDR, a rapid eye movement desensitization therapy that never worked with me until I tried it at West Coast.

I hated having to talk about all my experiences in front of strangers and I am sure they were not comfortable doing it either. It did not take long for me to realize that I was the most messed up in the group. I had tragedy after tragedy. I could tell I was stunning the doctors and therapists and they finally had to stop me because there were simply too many events to deal with.

I experienced a wide range of emotions during my stay. One of them was anger. I knew I was in trouble because the desire to be out of this world was still very strong. I expressed that in session and some of the therapists and doctors came off their chairs. I didn't care and I told them so. They didn't let me get away with it.

It was the sudden collision like into a brick wall that snapped me out of it and it was the best way for me. I was not expecting it. I was quickly told, "This isn't about you!" (like don't be so selfish). Another one said, "Would you die for your family?" I said, "of course." As soon as I said that, he said, "Then why can't you live for them, too?"

It was at that very instant that I realized how long ago I actually stopped thinking or caring about my family. I was on such a downhill slide that I passed them up at 100 mph. They had not even entered my thoughts for years. I did not care about what would happen to them once I was gone. **I just wanted out!**

This hit me like a rock. It was at this moment that the switch flipped, and the Lord showed me where I was and where I was really headed and the damage I had done.

I had arrived there so exhausted and worn out from not sleeping, that I landed in the local hospital for two days with pneumonia. The lead doctor and therapist checked on me. By this time, I had the major breakthrough and was highly motivated to get back.

During the coming days, everything we learned made perfect sense, but I still had one more big pill to swallow.

Toward the end of our next-to-last day, they showed a video of a police sergeant giving his last shift briefing. He looked very worn and haggard from the many years of dealing with the streets and watching after his people and all the stress and strain that came with it.

He was known to some of the doctors and therapists in the room. He had been meaning to retire. Those above and below him were after him to retire. He had been experiencing health problems. Despite his coworkers' concern and prodding, he felt he needed to keep going. Just a few more percent, a little while longer. He put it off for several years, passed what he should have. When he finally faced it and was facing retirement, his coworkers made an awesome video of his last day. It was really cool and it was what I hoped my last day would be like. As the video ended, the lead doctor said this sergeant died two weeks later from a massive heart attack.

He then looked down at me (he was tall and I was sitting up front) and in front of the whole class, therapists, **and** peers, he said, "Barba, this is you if you don't get out of this business immediately. You have a year or less to live if you don't from the massive heart attack heading your way."

I think he even offered to put it in writing. I knew he was right. I felt it deep inside, but I responded, "I can't retire. I have sixteen more months until I'm fifty."

He never broke eye contact with me and said, "Would you rather be dead?"

He went on to point out that I had a lot to live for, especially my family. For the first time in a long time, I fully agreed. He was trying to say I needed to retire on a psychological disability, but I still had an objection.

I shared the shame and extreme loneliness from going on the rubber gun squad and the humiliation I felt for four-and-a-half years. I shared my heavy sense of duty, honor, and code of conduct that was keeping me on. I also said that if I went that route, my family and I would lose all of our medical insurance and that it was my one big personal goal to service retire on my terms at fifty. I vowed I would not go passed fifty. His response was still the same, but pointed out the choice was mine. I did agree to take an extended time off work to think about it and to visit a neuropsychologist in Oakland on my way home.

She already had my info and, not surprisingly, had the same view as the doctors at West Coast. She wrote a letter taking me off work for an extended period of time and I was pretty much in tears when I gave it to my commander. He was not surprised and was very shook up when he had me sign the paper removing my peace officer powers, my departmental ID card, my service weapon, and my badge.

Once again, my whole identity was gone, but something was different this time. Yes, I was sad. However, the Lord came alongside me and showed me all that I had to live for and He had not forgotten me. He told me this was something else He would bring me through and I would use this for Him someday.

The following months were lonely. There is a very high degree of secrecy for those who attend programs like West Coast. Normally, word gets out within days that someone is out on stress or some other sort of disability.

I started getting nervous and thought maybe I should get an attorney like last time, but somebody who would really care. I found a lawyer who was the top in LA and was used by all the major fire and police departments. He agreed to see me.

I was nervous sitting in his office with my wife. He was an awesome guy and very honest. He said he could not help me because I had previously retired on stress and any award he got for me, my previous amount would be deducted, and he would end up working for free. He did give me the name and number of a highly recommended psychiatrist who would take over as my state comp treating physician.

I walked out of there extremely depressed and dejected. My wife actually put her arm around me, which didn't happen often. Talk about feeling alone!

However, true to His promise, I didn't feel alone for long. The Lord gave me an overwhelming feeling in my heart that all I needed was Him. He gave me the motivation to call my case manager at SCIF and tell her upfront that I wanted to take some time off, but then return to full duty and service retire. She was surprised but agreed. Even though I was bounced around to different case managers, I always found favor with them, and they were there every step of the way.

I called the doctor the attorney referred me to and even though he only took patients who were represented by attorneys, he took me as a patient.

During my first appointment with him, he sat across the desk from me and guided me via questions.

After just a few minutes of talking, he said "You're done. You will never go back to law enforcement again."

As to the havoc all this was wreaking in my home, he said, "I know you may not believe this now, but the problem is mostly you."

I wasn't ready for that and would have disagreed if it had been said to me one month earlier. However, at the rate the Lord was moving in my life, I took a while to think about it and I could finally see it.

As far as immediate retirement went, I pled my case as I had at West Coast. It met with pretty much the same response. The doctor also said that PTSD never goes away. This doctor was and I believe still is tops in his field. He was very strong and was always ready with answers and insight.

He subcontracted me out to an associate of his who was geographically 150 miles closer but remained my doctor of record with checkups every other month.

The doctor he farmed me out to was another awesome guy. I felt very blessed, and I firmly believe it was the Lord's way of showing me He was in control. I met weekly with him and was able to make good progress. He was very open to and supportive of putting the Lord first in my recovery and giving Him the praise and honor due Him for it. He was also not in favor of me ever going back to the department but was open as I progressed.

Life went on and I had to go into the station every couple of months to sign paperwork. There were only three sergeants, including myself at this small station. I was out for an unknown amount of time, and another sergeant was on vacation or out for a while.

Even in small offices, the workload can be immense. I felt bad because the only other sergeant stuck there was an old friend of mine who himself came back from medical retirement. We had known each other for twenty years and actually had common off-duty interests.

One particular day, I walked in and began small talk with him. He wouldn't look at me.

He just kept looking down at his desk, muttering over and over, "We'll get by, we'll get by."

As I attempted to talk to him and remind him how far back we went, he just kept looking down muttering the same thing, but then began to shake almost like a seizure with what appeared to be rage.

Our commander was out and he was acting commander, a role he loved. I could feel myself getting anxious all over again and all the physical and mental manifestations began to come back. I guess he was angry because, for the first time in years, I was starting to look and feel better. I think he felt I should have been at work, but had no inkling what was involved in my road back.

Within a couple of days, he was giving shift briefing with the outgoing shift also there. He proceeded to tell everyone what was going on with me, the nature of my leave of absence, and that I wasn't doing any of them any favors.

I heard about it within hours, and I began to brood. My feelings turned to anger and payback. I knew that if I filed a complaint with the sector chief for what this guy did, he would be rung up for a big HIPPA violation and fired or forced to retire. I also thought about filing another stress claim against him and the department.

Only three things kept me from doing it:

1. Our commander was out and already had his own plate full.
2. The memory of him as a friend.
3. I knew God was in control and it was in His hands.

For the first time, it felt great to just let go, and I have never regretted it.

The guy sent me a text a year or so later, trying to apologize, but just couldn't bring himself to do it. I knew life in the Buellton station after this was going to be awkward, at best. There was a large load for the sergeants to do and I really wanted to come back to work but not in Buellton. As it turned out, my commander needed someone to be there, and I was still a couple of months from being released to full duty. He called me to check on me, but he also was trying to ask if I would transfer to another station so he could get a warm body in there. He was just too good of a guy to come right out and ask so he stumbled around the subject a little.

I came right out and asked him if he wouldn't mind if I transferred back to King City. He sounded so relieved; it was actually a very funny moment.

Guide to Surviving in the Line of Duty

It took all I had to tell my commander where I was and to make the necessary phone calls to get in line for West Coast. My commander and our association could not have been better in contacting the right people to get me into the program.

The West Coast Post Trauma Retreat was a six-day in-patient program for first responders who are at the end of the line. The doctors and clinicians are all former cops and firefighters who are on a second career. You are surrounded by 10-20 peers. These are also first responders who have gone through trauma and the program.

I knew I was in the right place and that this is where God wanted me because He was to use it as part of my testimony.

> **For the first time, it felt great to just let go, and I have never regretted it.**

Read 1 Peter 5:7.

Are you on a collision course like I was?

Are you struggling with certain areas of your life and know you need help but do not know where to turn?

How would you answer the two questions that began to snap me out of it: "Would you die for your family?"

"Then why can't you live for them, too?"

Chapter 8

Retirement

I GOT MY TRANSFER BACK TO KING CITY. IT was all I could think of and my biggest goal was to see the words, "HONORABLY RETIRED," across the top of my badge. I asked the Lord to please let me finish strong. I said, "Lord, You have brought me through so much and I am a better man for it and there is something mighty You want me to do for You to help others who are going through deep water. Please let Your work be crowned by an honorable service retirement."

The commander of King City was a very close friend. We had been sergeants together and he was also in the twilight of his career. When the time came to go back, he did make it clear that I would be just as accountable as the other sergeants, so there were no special favors. I was very grateful and I knew the Lord was in it because I would have to work hard to the end.

In total, I had been off another fourteen months. Rarely is anything easy or fast in this business. In order to retake the field, I would have to attend another month plus a refresher at the CHP academy.

I arrived for what I knew would be my final training with an indescribable joy in my heart that can only come from one source. The Lord restored me, gave me joy, determination, and a purpose.

I walked around the 600-acre campus meeting a few friends I had worked with a few years before. One particular day, at lunchtime, I just wanted to go back to my dorm room and take a nap. However, something kept nagging at me to go up to the administration building to take care of something very minor.

I walked through the back-office area and said hello to a few instructors I knew. As I walked by a corner cubicle, I heard my name called. I looked over and saw someone I did not recognize. He was very thin and he could not hold still. He was also out of uniform wearing normal clothes. I acknowledged whoever it was, but I still did not recognize him. I had to walk within 3-4 feet of him to finally realize who it was.

It was "Phil"! We had worked together there at the academy for the better part of two years. He was a close friend and worked in the staff office (the equivalent of a drill instructor). He looked terrible! Super thin, shaking, and it looked like he hadn't slept in a long time. Phil told me he was going through a very bad divorce and custody battle, was under investigation by the department, and was possibly going to be terminated. All he was allowed to do was sit in that corner cubicle all day long and only leave for lunch and bathroom breaks.

When you are under investigation for serious offenses, you are not allowed to talk to anyone (including a mental health professional) about it other than your association/labor representative.

I understand the confidentiality of certain things, but what if you are completely innocent or if it was a shooting with lots of trauma and bloodshed? What if you were at the end of the road or already overwhelmed before this event? You are continually admonished not to discuss any details until the investigation is over and sometimes beyond that. Some find themselves in just this predicament and a few resort to suicide to escape.

Phil was trying to make small talk, but I could tell he was in a very dark place.

I interrupted him and said, "What are you carrying?"

He broke down and all the junk started to pour out of him. I suspected he was seriously considering suicide.

As I sat there with him, I became angry. I watched all these coworkers of his, uniformed officers and sergeants who had worked the streets, just walk right by him and completely ignore the fact he was crying. He had been banished to this spot and been in this sort of condition for some time. He said it was as if he was invisible. His own coworkers virtually ignored him and would walk by several times a day. A few would say hello, but others would go out of their way not to make eye contact.

This goes right back to my earlier point that with first responders, if you are in trouble, on the rubber gun squad, or under investigation, it seems that you look around you to find nobody there. Just like my rear gazelle analogy when the lions come. The rear gazelle is abandoned by the others and left to die. Phil's coworkers knew he was in distress, guilty or not, and he was hurting. Yet, he had been just left to sit. Maybe some feared they would be seen as violating the confidentiality around his case. Fine.

However, what is wrong with asking the three words, "Are you okay?" When you see a brother or sister struggling, please, at least ask. The struggle is not a contagious disease. If you are unable to get yourself to ask, find somebody who will and who will do something about it. Galatians 6:2 says we are to bear one another's burdens. You never know the difference it can make.

A young officer walked by who Phil and I had actually trained as a cadet at the academy. I grabbed him and told him to stay with Phil and not let him out of his sight. I walked into the lieutenant's office and told him what was happening. He seemed genuinely concerned and was able to get our peer support unit to our location within minutes.

As things turned out, just before I walked in, Phil was getting ready to go home for lunch and take his own life. Just a few days before, he had arranged for his dad to take care of his two young children, ages three and six. Phil's command staff got peer support out and peer support got him straight into West Coast Post Trauma Retreat. With the Lord's help, they were able to give him a new lease on life.

Just a couple of years later, Phil called me and wanted to say thanks for caring enough to ask where his mind was, get others involved, and get him to West Coast. He was enjoying his kids and life and was moving on in a very positive direction.

My heart melted even as I was on the phone with him. I felt so unworthy, but thanked him for the honor of helping him. The Lord then took it up one more notch. The feeling came into my heart and mind, "Where would Phil and his kids be if I had done the same thing Phil was thinking about so many years earlier?"

I thanked God then and I praise Him now that His word to me was fulfilled that He would use me and the hell on earth I had experienced to help others. I give God the glory and all the credit and praise. You may say that you will not know what to say to someone who is in Phil's position, but God says in Luke 12:12, "The Holy Spirit will give you the words to say at the moment when you need them." He has done this over and over in my life. People I have talked to have come to Christ and I had no idea what to say except under my breath, "God give me the words and prepare their hearts, minds, and ears to hear." It works. It truly works.

My Last Eight Months

I returned to the field and finished out my last eight months on the CHP. I was asked repeatedly if I wanted a retirement party. I was very grateful but declined each time. I wanted to go out the same way I came in—with no attention called to me. The office did a very small lunch with just a few people which was more my speed and very nice. No speeches!

My last day came on November 3, 2015. It was pouring rain all day. I was out backing up my folks and found myself directing traffic at an injury crash on the 101 freeway for a few hours. The Coastal Division Chief came to give me my retirement certificate and to say my last official goodbye.

He walked into the King City office and asked, "Where's Barba?"

The office staff said, "Out doing traffic control."

They finally had to call me back in over the radio. I had long ago cleaned out my desk and locker so I could change out one more time and go home.

I was very grateful to the chief and even more to those that worked for me and with me. The office was empty except the clerks and two desk officers and my commander. Everyone was still out at the crash. I walked back to an empty locker room, **ripped off my uniform, and ran out the door!**

The whole time I was gearing down, I was thanking and praising God for keeping His hand of protection upon me and being my silent partner for all the years.

As I drove home, I stopped at the store and bought my wife a huge bouquet of flowers and listened to the song, "18 Wheels and a Dozen Roses" by Kathy Mattea. I told the older cashier at the store I had just retired from the CHP and the flowers were for my wife. She started crying, in a good way. I got home and gave them to my wife with a kiss and thanked her for putting up with me for so long.

I am now over five years retired and love it. God continues to bless me in many ways. I enjoy my daughters and have seen one daughter marry and give me a granddaughter to spoil. He still brings me occasional first responders through word of mouth or by accident. My testimony works its way out and I always give God the glory.

One of the psychiatrists I saw told me, "Dan, PTSD never goes away." I have to say I still get the occasional flashback or dream. However, when you are redeemed in the Lord, those flashbacks and dreams serve as a positive reminder of what He has brought you through. If you use them to help and to witness to others, they give you a feeling that you could attack hell with a squirt gun.

Test God if you doubt it, but it starts with our own salvation. Through salvation, God puts the burden on our hearts for others, particularly those around us who are suffering. If you are a first responder, you are in a vast mission field with so very few workers. God can heal your life and set you on high while at the same time, use you to reach such a closed society as ours.

Please, give Him a chance. You have nothing to lose and an eternity with the Lord and those you win to Him to gain.

Guide to Surviving in the Line of Duty

I asked the Lord to please let me finish strong. I said, "Lord, You have brought me through so much and I am a better man for it and there is something mighty You want me to do for You to help others who are going through deep water. Please let Your work be crowned by an honorable service retirement." The Lord restored me, gave me joy, determination, and a purpose.

Read Galatians 6:2.

This says we are to bear one another's burdens and you never know the difference it can make.

When you see a brother or sister struggling, will you please at least ask them, "Are you okay?".

Retirement

God says in Luke 12:12, "The Holy Spirit will give you the words to say at the moment when you need them."

God has done this over and over in my life. People I have talked to have come to Christ and I had no idea what to say except under my breath, "God give me the words and prepare their hearts, minds, and ears to hear." It works. It truly works.

One of the psychiatrists I saw told me, "Dan, PTSD never goes away." I have to say I still get the occasional flashback or dream. However, when you are redeemed in the Lord, those flashbacks and dreams serve as a positive reminder of what He has brought you through. If you use them to help and to witness to others, they give you a feeling that you could attack hell with a squirt gun.

Chapter 9

THE SITUATION AT HOME

I REALLY DON'T WANT TO INCLUDE THIS, BUT this whole thing would seem incomplete if I left it out. Wonderful endings are for Hollywood movies, but the Lord can work it together for His good.

Having said that, my wife and I are still trying to make it work, even six years after retirement. When we married, we were of different faiths. Kind of similar, kind of not. If we had prayer together, it was rare and short. I did not like having devotional time because it always led to a fight. I remember feeling very alone while at church. I would see couples and families together who seemed happy. I saw older couples hold hands looking very much in love. I remember my heart actually aching because all I wanted was a happy home.

Going through what I went through gave me very thin skin. I perceived my wife as cold, uncaring, unable, or unwilling to relate to even the smallest thing.

Throughout the worst years of my career, I would and still do sweat profusely, especially in crowds or stressful situations. For over the last twenty years, I have woken up at night with my shirt soaked or very wet. My wife would say it was because I was overweight.

Trying to talk to her about what was happening inside me and then with us became impossible. With her inability to relate and me feeling like I was constantly under a heavy cross-examination in court, I would bite her head off and verbally viciously attack her. Soon, I would not even bother talking with her.

I moved out of our bedroom shortly after retiring and am in my own separate room to this day. It was mostly because of my snoring and tossing and turning (though we still have a disagreement about the cause).

For the most part, it was both of us not taking the time in the Word, praying, keeping ourselves focused on the Lord, and holding onto each other when things got bad. We just turned inward and really let the enemy put a huge wedge between us. We allowed it to go on for so long that things became almost irretrievably lost.

For the most part, it's always the families that pay the worst price. We all tend to bring things home with us. It is too heavy of a burden, but we need to leave it at the foot of the cross.

Surviving in the Line of Duty

> First responder, let your family comfort you and help you through things as they come. Don't take things out on them!
>
> Families, don't let your first responder isolate themselves. Hold them up in prayer. Lay hands on them daily and pray for the protection of the shed blood of Christ.

Conclusion

THE AGE OF DEFUND

IF A MEMBER OF THE GENERAL PUBLIC READS my story, they will be blown away by the amount of trauma, tragedy, and garbage I have shared. However, my experience is quite average, in my view. Most people have no idea that most of our law enforcement and other first responders walk around with their stress meter pegged. We are expected to clean up scenes, hold dead children, make life and death decisions in a split second, take abuse and blame from ignorant and radical members of the public and the media, and sometimes abuse from our own. Then we are to try to go home and be normal and have a normal life.

If there is a problem or a mental meltdown bringing danger to others, the feeling seems to be to give it to the cops. We are expected to solve it all and then get painted with the same brush when a rogue officer thousands of miles away or even right next door does something completely reprehensible.

I am constantly approached by young people wanting help getting into law enforcement. Lately, I have been telling them to go become a firefighter because people are always happy to see you. The near disappearance of support and the targeting by politicians and anarchists trying to bring this country down, along with everything else I have mentioned in this book makes a picture-perfect case for staying out of law enforcement, permanently.

If they persist, I let them know if this is the road they want to go down, they need a few things.

- A servant's heart: We are called to serve the public no matter what.
- Be willing to die and forfeit all you have here on this earth for someone who hates you.
- Give past what you have the capacity to give and still function.
- The most important thing is you must have Jesus Christ as your personal Lord and savior.
- You need to be on your knees each day or the job will bring you to them.
- If you are stuck and are too young to get out or too old for anything else, hold onto God all the more. He will get you and your family through

anything, but you must keep your eyes on the Lord constantly.

When Christ's disciples were in a boat going to meet Him, they encountered a rough storm. They felt they were all going to die until they saw Jesus walking on the water coming out to meet them.

Peter said, "Lord, if that is you bid me to come out to you."

Jesus said, "Come."

Peter got out of the boat and actually began walking on the water himself.

The Bible says that Peter soon realized what he was doing, where he was, and took his eyes off Jesus, he immediately began to sink.

Jesus calmly reached down and pulled him out and said, "You of little faith, why did you doubt?"

If you choose this profession of the first responder or it chooses you, never take your eyes off Him and stay under His protection. The Lord has delivered me from the brink and He will deliver you, as well. No matter where you are and no matter what you have faced or are facing, **He will do it**. All you have to do is ask. He can turn your tears and hurts into joy. He can take that joy even higher by using you to reach others who are in the same circumstances.

Every once in a while, I still get some of the symptoms, but they are no longer harmful and intrusive. They no longer do any damage. They are now gentle in nature and are reminders of what God has brought me through and how He has delivered me out of the morass and the slimy pit.

Psalm 40:2 says, "The Lord heard my cry and lifted me out of the slimy pit."

He is waiting to lift you.

Your deliverance can start today if you pray this simple prayer to Him:

Dear God,

I admit I am a sinner and need Your forgiveness. I believe that Jesus Christ died for my sins, paying the penalty for my sins. I am willing now to turn from my sin and accept Jesus Christ as my personal Lord and Savior. I commit myself to You and ask You to send the Holy Spirit into my life, to fill me, take control, and help me become that kind of person You want me to be. Thank You, Father, for loving me. In Jesus' name, Amen.

Now, pray for your family:

Dear God,

I bring You my family, (say their names, even though he already knows). I pray for Your cleansing blood that has the power to heal anything. I pray for their protection and for You to speak to their hearts, minds, and ears. Please restore us and bring Your precious love and bind us back together again with cords that cannot be broken. Help us to live for You and to seek Your face together. Use us in a great and mighty way. Thank You, Lord. In Your name, Amen.

This is **not** an effort to pull you into any denominational box. This is just plain simple salvation through Christ, no matter if you are a first responder or not. If you simply identify with what you have read and **are** at the end of the road, whether you realize it or not, you need Christ. He is the only answer. He can get you and your family through this. He can put your family back together. You may have tried everything else up until now and nothing has worked. Why not give Him a try? The fact that you have done me the honor of staying this far in this book shows that Christ is speaking to your soul.

If you do accept Him, find a good church where your spirit feels fed. Get into God's Word and let it talk to you. Don't just let someone like me tell you what the Bible says, read it for yourself. Let the promises come true in your own life.

I also firmly believe the Lord uses doctors and medications to help us. I highly encourage you to seek professional help from licensed therapists and doctors or clergy. A great start is places that specialize with broken, first responders, who may have been in one too many scrimmages without our helmets on; Places like West

Coast Post Trauma Retreat. They take first responders from all over the nation. Do **not** let any kind of cost stand in the way. Many have ways to work with you and even your employer.

The bottom line, let God be in the details. He will not only restore you, but He can set you even higher than you were. You have no idea how great life can be.

Thank you for the honor and privilege of walking through my story.

APPENDIX

Santa Barbara Law Enforcement Agents Lauded
Eight Awarded for Valor, Nine for Superior Performance
By **Adriana Zyskowski**

Sat, May 31, 2008: Recipients of the Superior Performance Award included Agent **Milt Baldwin** from the Lompoc Police Department, Officer **Daniel Barba** from the Santa Barbara division of the California Highway Patrol, Deputy D.A. **Mary Barron** from the Santa Barbara County District Attorney's Office, Detective **Jose Borrayo** from the UCSB Police Department, Sr. Juvenile Institutions Officer **Erin Cross** from the Santa Barbara County Probation Department, Officer **Ryan DeJohn** from the Santa Barbara Police Department, Officer **Steve Fulmer** from the Buellton division of the California Highway Patrol, Commander **Thomas Jenkins** from the Santa Barbara Sheriff's Department, and Officer **Gary Steigler** from the Santa Maria Police Department.

The H. Thomas Guerry Valor and Superior Performance Awards are given annually in honor of Santa Barbara City Police Officer H. Thomas Guerry, who died on January 3, 1970, at the age of 29 in the line of duty during an armed robbery near State and Ortega Streets.[4]

---

[4] https://www.independent.com/2008/05//31/santa-barba-law-enforecemen-agents-lauded/

CPSIA information can be obtained
at www.ICGtesting.com
Printed in the USA
LVHW110046191021
700772LV00004B/115